# THE OTHER

# SIDE

# OF THE

# DESK

A Guidebook to Surviving

and Thriving Your First Years

as a Secondary Teacher

JAIME BONATO

EVERGREEN
AUTHORS

*The Other Side of the Desk: A Guidebook to Surviving and Thriving Your First Years as a Secondary Teacher*

Copyright © 2021 by Evergreen Authors

ISBN: 978-1-954108-05-9

First printing in 2021
Printed in the United States of America

EVERGREEN AUTHORS
Minneapolis, Minnesota

# CONTENTS

# INTRODUCTION

Welcome to teaching! I am so excited you picked up this book, but I'm even more excited that you chose to be a teacher. I still remember my first years teaching (twenty years ago) as thrilling, scary, and exhausting. Pretty much any emotion you *can* feel, you probably *will* feel during the first year or two of teaching.

This book is designed for teachers who are currently enrolled in a teacher preparation program, teachers who are preparing for their first year, and new teachers who are currently teaching. As a new teacher mentor and teacher preparation educator, I have found some common themes among what new teachers want to know. This book is a concise, manageable length and filled with actionable items, but it's not so overwhelming that it will cause you anxiety and make you want to close it and leave it on your bookshelf. In short, it is a starting point—something to get you through designing your first year—but definitely not the last place you will look for ideas as you develop as a teacher.

In writing this book, I designed it as I would a course. The overall goal is that by working through this guidebook, you will envision what you want your classroom to be and then set up actionable steps to make that vision become reality. Each chapter has a topic, a focus for an outcome, and a practice piece (also known as homework). By the end of the book, you will have created a teacher binder that you can use to set up your classroom. If you start at the beginning of this book and work your way through, you will have a plan of action for your classroom, but you can also pop around the book to topics that are interesting to you or that you want to learn more about! Make this book work for you; there is no one right way to be a teacher, and you may modify the plan to fit your needs.

I am sending positive vibes your way as you read this and prepare for your class. Thank you for choosing to teach!

# UNIT 1

---

# Creating Your Classroom Vision

In this first unit, we will systematically walk through defining your classroom vision—a description of what you want for your classroom culture. Once you solidify this vision, you will develop a concrete plan to make it come to life, both physically and through clearly defined student and teacher expectations. The culminating product, which will be built through each chapter, is the framework for a teacher binder, a resource for you to refer to as you continue to plan.

# CHAPTER 1

---

# Visualizing the Dream Classroom

How do you create a clear vision for your classroom? What do you want your classroom vibe to be? How you want the classroom to "feel" to your students? In this chapter, I'll help you create this vibe through a classroom culture. You will also define goals for your students (beyond learning the curriculum) and big-picture ideas you want them to carry throughout life. This chapter will include brainstorming and thought-focusing activities to help you become crystal clear on what you want the essence of your classroom to be. This will lay the foundation for the rest of the book.

## Classroom Vibe

Think of a physical place that makes you feel good. It could be your bedroom, your grandparents' house, your favorite store at the mall, the beach, or someplace else that gives you a good feeling. Use your five senses when you think about this place. How does it smell? What is the temperature? What do you hear? The essence of a place impacts the vibe or emotional reaction you experience. Just as places like churches, shopping malls, or pet stores create a vibe, your classroom will have a vibe too.

---

*vibe* (n): a distinctive feeling or quality capable of being sensed[1]

---

Retailers spend millions of dollars creating vibes that influence shoppers' moods and emotions, which then influence the shoppers' behavior.[2] Just think about Starbucks stores. When you walk into any Starbucks, the atmosphere gives off a particular vibe. The temperature is usually complimentary to outside conditions (cool inside if it is warm outside and vice versa), the lighting is not too bright or too dark, there is chill music playing, food treats are on display, and there's usually a low hum of customers talking

---

[1] *Merriam-Webster, s.v.* "vibe (n.)," accessed May 21, 2020, https://www. merriam-webster.com/dictionary/vibe.

[2] Claus Ebster and Marion Garaus, *Store Design and Virtual Merchandising: Creating Store Space that Encourages Buying* (New York: Business Expert Press, 2011), 108.

or moving about. You also know what to expect. You will order at the counter, the items offered are the same at each location, and there will be an area to pick up your order when it is done. The physical environment, along with the procedures set in place to guide the customer through the experience, create a sense of calm.

Similarly, a classroom environment can influence students' comfort level, willingness to participate, stress and anxiety levels, and behaviors. When a classroom is emotionally stressful, it can reduce a students' ability to learn.[3] With this in mind, a classroom with a good vibe can relax students and make them feel more open to learning. Like Starbucks, your classroom can give behavior clues to students. If you want them to pick up a paper on their way in, leave the stack by the door. Have instructions clearly visible to let students know what to do. Arrange furniture so students will flow into and around the classroom easily.

Often, teachers put their policies and procedures in place on the first day of school and the classroom feeling follows. I am going to challenge you to instead build your classroom around a feeling and let the policies and

---

[3] Robert Sylwester, "How Emotions Affect Learning," *Educational Leadership*, October 1994, http://www.ascd.org/publications/education-al-leadership/oct94/vol52/num02/How-Emotions-Affect-Learning.aspx.

procedures follow (don't worry—we will talk about policies and procedures thoroughly in a future chapter). We are going to narrow down what you want your classroom vibe to be through a quick exercise.

## EXERCISE

Recall your most memorable teachers, classes, and classrooms—both good and bad. Take three minutes to write down why these teachers, classes, and classrooms are memorable. Some questions to consider: What did the classroom look like? What stood out to you about the class? What feeling did you have as you walked into the room?

After you have jotted some names and reasons down, go back and circle the key ideas that stand out. Write a feeling next to your circled key ideas. Reflect on how the teacher made you feel as a student. Good, bad, ugly, whatever it is, you will want to remember these feelings as you create your classroom.

Look back at the big feelings you pulled out of the above exercise. Some of the feelings you may have identified are:

- Relaxed
- Energetic
- Calm
- Trusting
- Peaceful
- Intense

- Excited
- Critical
- Anxious
- Serene

- Oppressive
- Depressing
- Repressive
- Nervous

Choose three feelings that you want you and your students to experience in your classroom. Jot them on a paper, in the lines below, on a sticky note, or somewhere else you can refer back to.

_____

_____

_____

Now you have identified the feelings you want students to have when they come into your classroom. Let's talk about how to create a class culture to support these feelings.

## Creating a Classroom Culture

Once you have defined your classroom vibe and the emotions you hope it will evoke in students, you will need to design a plan for creating a class culture to support all of your students. The term *culture* is defined as "the characteristic features of everyday existence (such as diversions or a way of life) shared by people in a place or time."[4] Classroom culture refers to the way things are done, the way people interact with each other, and the shared practices in a classroom. Earlier, you described the *vibe* you want your classroom to have. The *culture* is how that vibe plays out and what you and your students do to create that vibe.

To establish a classroom where students are emotionally available to learn, they must be comfortable and feel valued and included. "Creating a positive environment produces a powerful ripple effect that continually enhances learning: when students can see the humor in their mistakes, celebrate their successes, and feel empowered as change agents, they will actively engage in learning and, consequently, learn more effectively."[5]

There are many books and classes on creating classroom culture, but for the purposes of this chapter, I will give a brief overview of some areas you can focus on to create a positive classroom culture.

---

[4] *Merriam-Webster*, s.v. "culture (n.)," accessed May 21, 2020, https://www.merriam-webster.com/dictionary/culture.

[5] Joan Young, *Encouragement in the Classroom:* How Do I Help Students Stay Positive and Focused? (Alexandria, VA: ASCD Arias, 2014), [2].

## LEARN ABOUT THE COMMUNITY

The first way to create a positive culture in your classroom is to honor your students' experiences. Students come from many different backgrounds. Before the school year begins, research the community where your school is located. The website Teaching Tolerance suggests that teachers learn about neighborhood demographics, strengths, and concerns.[6]

## THINK ABOUT WHAT YOUR CLASSROOM LOOKS LIKE

When you set up your classroom, be mindful of what you put on the walls as decoration or educational content. In a 2014 journal article, researchers describe how there is evidence that students use the visual appearance of a classroom to draw inferences about the classroom's culture.[7] The visual appearance of a classroom can signal to students whether they will be valued as a member of the class.

---

[6] "Critical Practices for Anti-bias Education," Teaching Tolerance, accessed May 21, 2020, https://www.tolerance.org/magazine/publications/critical-practices-for-antibias-education.

[7] Sapna Cheryan, Sianna A. Ziegler, Victoria C. Plaut, Andrew N. Meltzoff, "Designing Classrooms to Maximize Student Achievement," *Policy Insights from the Behavioral and Brain Sciences* 1, no. 1 (October 1, 2014): 4–12, https://doi.org/10.1177/2372732214548677.

With this in mind, selectively decide what you will put on the walls. Ask yourself if your classroom represents the students who will learn there. I always lean toward a minimally decorated classroom at first, then fill the walls as the year progresses. Information relevant to students, such as school bulletins and bell schedules, should be posted in an accessible spot. Posters with inspirational quotes and suggestions on mindfulness can also fill the walls. Be cautious when decorating with a specific theme, such as your favorite sports team, book, or movie. Students may not share your enthusiasm, and your classroom might feel unwelcoming to them.

When in doubt about decorating your classroom, remember that less is more. Too much visual stimulation has been shown to distract students and inhibit their learning.[8] And remember that while it's worthwhile to search websites like Pinterest for classroom decorating ideas, your classroom does not need to be "Pinterest perfect!"

---

[8] Anna V. Fisher, Karrie E. Godwin, Howard Seltman, "Visual Environment, Attention Allocation, and Learning in Young Children: When Too Much of a Good Thing May Be Bad," *Psychological Science* 25, no. 7 (May 21, 2014): 1362–70, https://doi.org/10.1177/0956797614533801.

## LISTEN TO YOUR STUDENTS

Ask your students what they want their classroom to be like. What do they value? What helps them learn and what hinders their learning? After you pose a question, truly listen to your students' answers. Create a space where students feel comfortable expressing themselves. The best way to encourage all students to respect and support each other is by modeling respectful behavior. When creating classroom expectations and norms (we will talk about this in the next chapter), allow students to have input.

## RESPECT YOUR STUDENTS

I am a firm believer that respect is a two-way street. I would never expect my students to respect me if I did not extend them the same courtesy. One of the most important ways to show respect is to learn how to pronounce each student's name. Incorrectly pronouncing a student's name sends the message that you may disregard the student's culture and background.[9] Taking the time to correctly pronounce a student's name can make a student

---

[9] Clare McLaughlin, "The Lasting Impact of Mispronouncing Students' Names," NEA News, *NEA Today*, September 1, 2016, https://www.nea. org/advocating-for-change/new-from-nea/lasting-impact-mispronouncing-students-names.

feel welcomed and honored in the classroom.[10] Students should also be encouraged and expected to learn and pronounce each other's names correctly.

## Enduring Understanding: What Students Really Remember

Enduring understandings are big ideas you want students to take away from your class. Often, enduring understandings are content-driven. For example, when teaching writing, an enduring understanding could be, "Writers must make choices about how to structure their writing based on its intended purpose." For now, put the content understanding on hold and think about the big ideas you want your students to take with them when they leave your class at the end of the year.

When a group of professors was asked what they wanted their students to remember from their class, none of them mentioned content. Instead, the common theme was hope that the course would help students live better

---

[10] Corey Mitchell, "A Teacher Mispronouncing a Student's Name Can Have a Lasting Impact," *PBS NewsHour*, PBS, May 16, 2016, https://www.pbs.org/newshour/education/a-teacher-mispronouncing-a-students-name-can-have-a-lasting-impact.

lives.[11] For right now, we are going to think about the big picture: what do you want your students to remember about learning in general when they leave your class? Here are a few examples:

- There is always more to learn, and I understand how to continue learning.
- There can be many points of view on a topic. I can be open to other viewpoints and come to my own conclusion.
- Mistakes are valuable and I can learn from them.
- It is okay to not be perfect, but it is not okay to not try.
- History is more complex than the general public believes it to be.
- There is joy in learning.
- I can critically think through a problem and justify a possible solution.

---

[11] James M. Lang, "What Will Students Remember from Your Class in 20 Years?," *The Chronicle of Higher Education*, September 30, 2018, https://www.chronicle.com/article/what-will-students-remember-from-your-class-in-20-years/.

- I will be a positive, contributing member of society who can form opinions based on many data points.

When I think of enduring understandings that I want students to take from my class, I think of those motivational posters you see in classrooms and offices. Spend about five minutes thinking about enduring understandings you want your students to have. If you are stuck, do an internet search for "motivational quotes." Choose two or three enduring understandings you want your students to leave your class with. Write these enduring understandings down on a piece of paper or in the margin of this book.

_____

_____

_____

_____

_____

## Write a Classroom Vision

Just like a school without a vision can lack direction,[12] a classroom without a vision can leave you detached from purpose and direction. Often, teachers get stuck in the small details of teaching, so having a big-picture reminder to refer back to can put those daily struggles in perspective. After you have honed in on what you want your classroom vibe to be, you will be able to create a classroom vision.

Many school districts or schools have vision statements. These can be great starting points, but your statement should be specifically targeted to your classroom. Take a moment to look up your district's or school's vision statement. If you like the vision statement, agree with its focus, and think it aligns with the enduring understandings you've chosen, you can adapt it to fit your classroom vision.

When you create your vision, you will want it to be concise and capture what you want students to aspire to during and after your class. Here are a few examples from the business world:

---

[12] John G. Gabriel and Paul C. Farmer, *How to Help Your School Thrive Without Breaking the Bank* (Alexandria, VA: ASCD, 2009), [45].

**17**

At IKEA our vision is to create a better everyday life for the many people. Our business idea
supports this vision by offering a wide range
of well-designed, functional home furnishing
products at prices so low that as many people
as possible will be able to afford them.[13]

Under Armour's vision is to inspire you with performance solutions you never knew you needed
and can't imagine living without.[14]

[LinkedIn's Vision:] Create economic opportunity
for every member of the global workforce.[15]

Notice that all of these vision statements go beyond
promoting a product or service; they focus on helping
people live fuller lives. Now think about that in light of
these examples of teachers' classroom vision statements.

[13] "Our Vision and Business Idea," IKEA, accessed November 18, 2020, https://www.ikea.com/ms/en_JP/about_ikea/the_ikea_way/our_busi-ness_idea/index.html.

[14] "About UA," Under Armour, accessed November 18, 2020, https://about.underarmour.com/.

[15] "About LinkedIn," LinkedIn, accessed November 18, 2020, https://about.linkedin.com/.

*Your vision does not have to be perfect. It can be tweaked and changed as you go through the school year. The important thing is that you have an overall idea of what you want students to take away from your classroom.

*Vision and mission statements often go hand in hand. Typically, a vision is the overarching idea and the mission gets more specific about the actions that realize the vision. For now, just focus on creating your vision.

My students will be 21st Century learners. They will be able to think critically about the curriculum and how it relates to their lives outside of the classroom. They will be able to communicate effectively with their peers, their teachers, the community, and the world. They will be able to collaborate and work well with others. And they will be creative in sharing what they have learned and their passions.[16]

My classroom will be a positive community of learners where the individual needs of all students are met, successes are celebrated, and students build character and skills which will make them productive citizens both today and in the future.[17]

When you create your own classroom vision statement, you can either work from scratch or use a vision statement that already exists. You can also start with one classroom vision statement and modify it to align with your classroom vibe, culture, and enduring understandings throughout the year. Remember, your vision does not have to include big words; in fact, it should be easily understandable for students.

---

[16] Melissa Hero, "My Classroom Vision and Mission Statements," *Moving Forward* (blog), August 15, 2016, http://mdhero.blogspot.com/2016/08/my-classroom-vision-and-mission.html.

[17] Pamela Snavely, "Mrs. Snavely's Mission Statement," *Washington Elementary, Mrs. Snavely's 4th Grade* (blog), accessed November 18, 2020, https://mrssnavelys4thgrade.weebly.com/classroom-vision-and-mission-statements.html.

*We teachers use each other's materials all the time. Do not hesitate to search out an already written vision statement and use it for your classroom.

Once your vision is ready, print it out and keep it in a place where you will see it often (perhaps in a lesson planner or hanging near your workspace). When the daily grind hits, you will be able to refer back to your bigger vision. When you reflect as the year goes on, you can ensure that your teaching practices align with your vision.

## Homework

Create your own classroom vision statement. Use the tips above and come up with a draft of your vision. Remember, your vision statement may change over time, and you can adjust it to meet the needs of your students. When you have found your classroom vision statement, write or print it our and display it somewhere you will see often while planning and teaching.

# CHAPTER 2

---

# Making Your Classroom Vision Come to Life

With your vision prepared, we can now turn our focus to bringing that vision to life in the classroom so your students can achieve it. This first thing this chapter will tackle is the physical setup of your classroom. You may not know yet what your classroom will look like, but it is helpful to have some basics in mind so when you do get your keys, you are ready to start setting up. You will also begin to create classroom expectations—the behaviors you want your students to exhibit during class. Finally, you will brainstorm and begin to plan classroom routines.

## Physical Classroom Setup

As a new teacher, you are especially susceptible to last-minute classroom switches. There have been tales of new teachers being moved to a completely different classroom the night before school started. Thinking about room arrangement can be a little abstract if you don't know what your classroom is going to look like or if you don't know whether you'll stay in your assigned room. However, you can get a few basic ideas ready of how you want your classroom physically laid out so that when you do get your room, you're ready to roll.

The physical classroom has been shown to influence student achievement,[18] and how you set up your classroom can have some control over this influence. There are many factors to consider when thinking about your physical classroom, including lighting, wall decorations, temperature, and desk arrangement.

## LIGHTING

The lighting in a room can affect students' moods, behaviors, and learning, according to a recent article by neuroscientist Melina Uncapher.[19] Ideally, a classroom

---

[18] Sapna Cheryan, Sianna A. Ziegler, Victoria C. Plaut, Andrew N. Meltzoff, "Designing Classrooms to Maximize Student Achievement," *Policy Insights from the Behavioral and Brain Sciences* 1, no. 1 (October 1, 2014): 4–12, https://doi.org/10.1177/2372732214548677.

[19] Melina Uncapher, "The Science of Effective Learning Spaces," *Edutopia*, October 14, 2016, https://www.edutopia.org/article/science-of-effective-learning-spaces-melina-uncapher.

should have a lot of natural light. If your classroom does not have ample natural light, Uncapher suggests replacing lightbulbs with blue-enriched bulbs. This is most likely not a realistic expense, but it may be something you can ask the custodial staff about. Another idea is to purchase decorative LED light coverings.

## NOISE

Noise inside the classroom is something you can control, but there will be times when you want a quiet environment for students to independently read, write, or process information while there is noise outside of your classroom that you cannot control. Traffic, P.E. classes running by, airplanes flying overhead, and other noises will occur during your class time. While outside sounds are impossible to control, you may be able to work around them. If you know that the landscaping crew will be outside every Tuesday around 9:00 am, don't plan quizzes or other activities that require quiet during that time. It is not always avoidable, but sometimes flipping when you offer quiet time is a doable solution.

Noise and sound can also be used to your advantage. If your class reacts well, consider playing instrumental music while students work independently or as they enter class. Noise machines (especially the ones that use white noise) may help cancel out unwanted noise outside of the classroom.

## TEMPERATURE

This is one factor that will very likely be out of your control. Many schools have thermostats in classrooms with preset temperature controls. Excessively hot classrooms can have a negative impact on student performance.[20] If you find that your room is too hot or stuffy, you can put fans in to help circulate the air. Often, custodians will have extra fans they can set up in your room.

## SMELL

With thirty or more people in a room for hours a day, there will most likely be a certain smell. Sometimes we are not aware that our classroom is smelly or stuffy because we are in it all day. To test the smell of your classroom, find another teacher to watch your students for five minutes. Run a quick campus errand or walk around the building, then reenter your room. How does it smell? There are ways to combat stinky classrooms (just Google "stinky

---

[20] Joshua Goodman, Michael Hurwitz, Jisung Park, Jonathan Smith. "Heat and Learning." NBER Working Paper Series (24639), National Bureau of Economic Research, Cambridge, MA, May 2018. https://www.nber. org/papers/w24639.

classroom"), but I find that keeping my classroom windows and door open between passing periods can help. Use caution when using deodorizers, since some students are allergic or very sensitive to aerosols or certain scents.

## DECORATIONS

Classroom decor and displayed objects can either hinder or improve student learning.[21] Be mindful that a visually busy or overly decorated classroom can cause overstimulation and actually impede learning.[22] When choosing what to place on the walls and throughout the classroom, remember that less is more. Make sure that whatever you display is inclusive and representative of the cultures of your students. Display objects that represent multiple social identities. According to the website Teaching Tolerance, "Classrooms should be decorated with multicultural images that mirror student backgrounds and

---

[21] Cheryan et. al.

[22] Anna V. Fisher, Karrie E. Godwin, Howard Seltman, "Visual Environment, Attention Allocation, and Learning in Young Children: When Too Much of a Good Thing May Be Bad," *Psychological Science* 25, no. 7 (May 21, 2014): 1362–70, https://doi.org/10.1177/0956797614533801.

showcase the diversity of our society."[23] Adding extra light sources and plants (real or fake—fake for me because I cannot keep plants alive) can also make a space feel more inviting.

Some teachers include a student information center or wall in their classroom. School schedules, calendars, and updates can be posted in this area. You might consider posting upcoming assignments and test dates in the same place so students become accustomed to knowing where to look for information. You can even post your class vision statement on the wall as a reminder to you and your students!

---

\* Make sure to follow all fire marshal guidelines and rules when you decorate!

---

When decorating your classroom, be mindful that the classroom is a shared learning space. If you have a particular theme you would like to design around, such as a specific book series, remember that some students

---

[23] "Critical Practices for Anti-bias Education Classroom Culture," Teaching Tolerance, accessed May 21, 2020, https://www.tolerance.org/magazine/publications/critical-practices-for-antibias-education/classroom-culture.

may dislike the series and feel alienated. For example, if you are a Harry Potter fan and decorate your classroom with all things Harry Potter, a student that does not connect with or hasn't read that series may not feel welcomed.

## FURNITURE ARRANGEMENT

Your classroom furniture arrangement will be an immediate signal to students about the culture of the classroom. Desk placement can help facilitate your classroom. However, your arrangement may be limited based on the size or layout of the classroom. For example, some science classrooms have fixed workstations, and some classrooms are set up in lecture halls. Play around with arrangements to find out what works best.

When arranging your classroom, think about how students will access supplies (rulers, paper, markers, scissors, etc.). If you have community supplies, think about storing them in an easily accessible, minimally distracting location.

## STUDENT DESK ARRANGEMENT

When a student walks into a classroom, the furniture arrangement, particularly the student desk arrangement, sends a message about students' and teachers' roles, as well as the degree of expected collaboration, dialogue, and ownership of the classroom.[24] When deciding the desk arrangement in the classroom, think about your goals. Do you want students to talk to each other in partners, small groups, or large groups? Do you want students to work on projects collaboratively? Your desk arrangement may change depending on the activity the class is working on. Sometimes there will be constraints on how you can arrange the desks based on the classroom size and layout. Get creative, or ask students to work with you.

Having desks in traditional rows is not inherently wrong, but if you want students to be able to move desks to work in groups or pairs, make sure it's possible ahead of time. If your seating arrangement is fluid, spend time up front training students on how to move their desks into different arrangements. Give clear and explicit instructions, such as, "if you are sitting in this row, your desk will turn this way."

## TEACHER DESK

The placement of your desk will also give a signal to students about classroom culture. A teacher's desk in the

---

[24] Ibid.

front and center of the room indicates that the teacher is the center of learning. To encourage students to feel that they are the center of learning, consider setting up your desk or workstation either in the back or to the side of the room.

Think about how you will present instruction. If you will be using technology, you may have to work near an outlet or within proximity to certain devices. Will you stand during instruction? Will you ever sit? Consider the height of your desk and if you will use a stool or a chair.

## CLASSROOM ACCESSIBILITY

The classroom needs to be accessible to all students. If you have students with disabilities who need extra accommodations, make sure your classroom has what they need. Think about the desks where students will be sitting, ensuring that walkways are accessible to all, and storing supplies where students have access. This can be very difficult, especially if your classroom is limited in size, but try to get creative. Walk around your classroom as if you were a student and see if everything you need is accessible. Sit in each desk and ensure you can see the teacher, the board, and the television (if you use one). If there is a station for student supplies, make sure it is organized and easy for students to access and return materials.

You can also ask students for seating preferences. Some students prefer to sit in the front of the room. Others are easily distracted by looking out a window and would benefit from a seat that limits this distraction. Ask your students what they think the classroom should look and feel like. Are they comfortable with the lighting, temperature, and desk arrangements? Ask them for ideas on how to improve. You don't have to use all of their ideas, but they may give you something to think about and possibly change.

## Creating Classroom Behavior Expectations

Classroom expectations describe overall student behavior, while classroom procedures and routines describe specific actions. As you create your expectations, think of overall student behaviors you want to see in the classroom. For example, "be respectful of everyone's property" is an expectation, while specific procedures, such as how students will pass forward or turn in their papers, is considered a procedure or routine. Future chapters will discuss procedures and routines in further detail, but for now, let's focus on expectations.

The following is a generic list of possible things to

include.[25] I recommend choosing at most five classroom expectations, so find the ones that encompass what you want most from students.

- Follow classroom rules.
- Be on time.
- Be prepared for class.
- Be considerate and respectful.
- Show respect for school property and other students.
- Hand in assignments on time.
- Wait to be dismissed.
- Use an inside voice.
- Actively participate in class discussions.
- Stay seated during classroom activities and events.
- Help each other.
- Work quietly and follow directions.
- Raise your hand before speaking.

---

[25] Janelle Cox, "Reasonable Expectations for Students: A Guide for New Teachers," ThoughtCo., January 24, 2020, https://www.thoughtco.com/student-expectations-for-beginning-teachers-2081937.

Some teachers add general ideas like "always try your best." I like to include these types of ideals in the classroom vision and use expectations for actions that, as a teacher, you are clearly able to assess. It may be difficult to assess if a student is truly trying their best, but it is easy to observe if they are not prepared for class. Still, "always try your best" is something all teachers want their students to do. I think that this is encouraged more through the relationships you develop with your students, not necessarily through the list of classroom expectations.

One year, in my high school classroom of mostly seniors, I decided to only have the expectation "be cool." I quickly learned that students needed to know in detail what "being cool" meant. For me, it was meant to encompass the idea of respect and basic classroom etiquette, such as not talking when others were talking, cleaning up after yourself, or not taking other people's things. Within a week, I had to create a list of specific expectations. I still left "be cool" as the main expectation, but I added a poster that I co-created with my students to more deeply describe what "being cool" was.

Whether or not you decide to create expectations as a group, it is important that you have an idea in mind of your non-negotiable expectations for student behavior. If you co-create expectations with your class, they will most likely come up with your non-negotiables on their own, but either way, make sure your expectations are included in any class-created list.

Depending on your students, the detail in which you must explain the expectations may vary. For example, let's say one of the expectations is "be respectful of everyone's property." When you introduce your expectations to the class, you may want to include a short discussion of what respecting everyone's property looks like. Specific examples could include "not taking something that doesn't belong to you without permission" or "returning classroom materials once you are done." If your class needs a lot of explicit instruction on their behavior, you may choose to add specific actions that exhibit your expectations. I try to start the year with broad expectations and then add examples later if the class is struggling with the concept.

Refer to the expectations frequently during the first few weeks of school. Students will need constant reminders and positive reinforcement. For example, if one of your expectations is "do not pack up before the end of class," you may thank students for not packing up as you're wrapping up your lesson.

As you create your classroom behavior expectations,

remember the vision you have for your classroom and the overall feel that you want your students to have when they're in the room. You may decide to change things about your physical classroom setup as you brainstorm classroom expectations and think about physical environments that may better support your expectations.

## Homework

Create a plan for your classroom's physical design. Look to other teachers' classrooms for inspiration. (Pinterest is a great resource—but remember, your classroom does not have to look Pinterest perfect!) First, take notes on how you will address the following:

- Lighting
- Noise
- Temperature
- Smell
- Decorations
- Furniture Arrangement
- Student Desk Arrangement
- Teacher Desk
- Classroom Accessibility

Next, develop a list of at most five classroom expectations. List them below. (Remember that these may change and evolve over time.)

1. _____

2. _____

3. _____

4. _____

5. _____

# CHAPTER 3

# Figuring Out the Lay of the School Land

Now that you have your classroom vision, the next step is laying the foundation to make it come to life! I know you want to start planning lessons, decorating your classroom, and diving right in, but taking the time to figure out the lay of the land will pay off as you get into the details of teaching. We are going to talk about the important people, places, and things you'll need to know. Once you have these down, you will know where to go to get help when you need it.

## Important People

There is a saying in teaching circles that the two most important people on campus are the secretary and the custodian. Find out who these people are and be very nice to them! (But don't just be nice because they can make your life miserable . . . be nice because these people have really tough jobs and often don't get the credit they deserve. Let them know how much you appreciate them and thank them for their help.) There are plenty of other people you will want to get to know because they are there to help you and your students succeed.

## SCHOOL SECRETARIES

School secretaries keep the school running smoothly. They can usually help you directly, or at least help you figure out where to get what you need. Over the years, my school secretaries have helped me figure out the substitute system, plan the logistics of field trips, fill out paperwork for attending conferences, and stay aware of important dates and school news. Introduce yourself to the school secretary before the school year starts and let them know you are new and may need a little extra help with some logistics.

## ATTENDANCE AND REGISTRAR

Depending on the size of the school, your site will most likely have someone dedicated to keeping track of student attendance and another person dedicated to student records. You will most likely know this person mainly through email, so stop by and introduce yourself in person.

## SCHOOL COUNSELOR(S)

Many schools have counselors dedicated to enrolling students in classes and offering emotional, academic, and mental support. The school counselor is a great resource for you and students. If you feel a student may need extra services, talk to a counselor for ideas and support. Before you meet your students, try to introduce yourself to the school counselor to establish a relationship.

## CUSTODIANS

I think school custodians are some of the most unappreciated school staff. Have you ever seen a cafeteria at the end of lunch?? Depending on the size of your school, your classroom might be assigned to a specific custodian. Be good to this person! If you have a class party with food, leave a little treat for the custodian. Always have your class pick up trash from the floor and do general cleanup to make the custodian's work easier. Your floors will be much cleaner if the custodian uses their time to vacuum or mop rather than pick up paper scraps and pencils. Also, be sure to thank the custodian for their work! A simple "thank you for all you do" as you pass them in the hall is a small gesture of gratitude, but it will be noticed.

## OTHER SITE TEACHERS

When you are starting out as a new teacher, the other teachers at your site can serve as your lifeline. They know the school culture and the curriculum. Use the resources other teachers are willing to share. Ask them about pacing, classroom management . . . anything! Your grade-alike teachers can help with curriculum, and teachers from lower grades can give insight about challenges you may face with upcoming classes of students. Teachers want other teachers to succeed, so ask for help!

---

*Observing other teachers during your off periods is a great way to learn more teaching techniques and practices. Most teachers will be more than happy to welcome you into their classrooms to observe!

---

Just remember that some teachers don't want to share *everything* with others, so you may want to approach your colleagues with, "are you willing to share…?" Also, sharing is a two-way street. Offer to share resources you have found with other teachers; as a veteran teacher, I love getting resources from a new teacher with a fresh perspective.

While most teachers will be helpful and enthusiastic about sharing their love of teaching, some teachers may be more cynical. Avoid teachers who constantly complain without offering solutions, trash-talk students and administrators, and have a general negative attitude toward teaching. You do not need to be rude to the morale draggers, but be cordial and instead seek out uplifting, respectful colleagues for in-depth conversations or general help.

## LIBRARIAN

Librarians are trained to support students and teachers. Many librarians will offer to teach lessons on research and other topics to your students. Take advantage of their offers! Librarians may also have access to funds to purchase books for the school library, so if you see a book you are interested in (teaching or otherwise), you could ask the librarian to buy it for the library and then check it out for yourself.

## ADMINISTRATORS
## (PRINCIPALS, VICE-PRINCIPALS)

It goes without saying that the administration—principals and vice-principals—are the captains of the school ship. Many times, the principal is the person who hired you for your teaching assignment, so they must see something great in you! I know these people may seem intimidating, especially since they're usually the ones who complete your official evaluation, but the administration team wants the school to be the best it can be—and they want you to be the best you can be. I suggest that after you exhaust your other resources (other teachers and librarians), ask for advice and help from the administration. Often, principals can either mentor you or direct you to resources that can best support you. You can also ask administrators for help before you ask others, but I find that many times my fellow teachers had the most immediate responses and real-time help.

### SCHOOL DISTRICT LEADERS

Many larger school districts have specific departments that focus on curriculum, instruction, and student support. These departments can often provide additional resources to support the school level curriculum. They may also offer professional development. Find out if your district has this type of support and be on the lookout for emails from this department or person about any training they may offer.

## HUMAN RESOURCES CONTACT

When you are hired, you will most likely do some intake paperwork, and there will be a point-of-contact person in the human resources office. Know this person's name (I used to look my person up every single time, and it wasted a lot of time). The human resources department can set up your direct deposit and insurance and answer any questions you may have. Also, double-check your first paycheck to make sure your information and payment are correct.

## PARENT ASSOCIATION

Many schools have parent-teacher associations (sometimes called PTO, PTA, or PTSA if they add "student" in the title). Often, these groups look for teachers to help. Remember this when you are gathering supplies and materials for your classroom. I also suggest attending at least the first meeting of the year so you can introduce yourself and meet the association's key players.

## Important Places

Get to know your school campus and where to find essentials as soon as you have access. Set aside an hour to locate the places you will use. Here is a list of places to become familiar with:

- Main office
- Supply room
- Teacher mailboxes
- Outgoing mailbox
- Library
- Faculty parking
- Restrooms (both teacher and student, so you know where your students go when they use a hall pass)
- Copier (also become familiar with how to use it!)
- Cafeteria
- Teachers' lounge
- Fire drill evacuation routes

## Important Things

To get and keep your classroom ready, you will need supplies and materials for you and your students. I've added both a list of recommended supplies and a list of ideas for where to get these supplies.

## SUPPLIES

*Teacher Supplies (keep these separate from class-room supplies):*

- Pens
- Pencils
- Highlighters
- Eraser
- White-out
- Binders
- Index cards

- Folders
- Sticky notes
- Stapler
- Staples
- Staple remover
- Paper clips
- Tape

*Classroom Supplies (to be used by students and teacher):*

- Pens
- Pencils
- Pencil sharpener
- Highlighters
- Pencil erasers
- Three-ring binders
- Composition notebooks

- Subject dividers
- Folders
- Graphing calculators (depending on subject)
- Notebook filler paper
- Stapler

- Staples
- Index cards
- Dry-erase markers
- Whiteboard eraser
- Paper clips
- Three-hole punch
- Copy paper
- Disinfecting wipes
- Facial tissues
- Hand sanitizer
- Tape

*Bonus Items (these can come in handy):*

- Plastic sandwich bags
- Portable whiteboards
- Painter's tape
- Chart paper
- Bins to collect papers

## GETTING SUPPLIES

Setting up your classroom for the first time can seem overwhelming, especially if your school does not have the basic classroom supplies (and let's face it . . . the starting salary for a new teacher doesn't leave a lot of cushion to buy supplies). This is where you can get creative. Below are a few places you can search for supplies at low to no cost:

*The school supply room.* If your school has a supply room or closet stocked with classroom supplies, check it out. Your principal, the school secretary, or the department chair may also be able to order some supplies for you.

*Thrift stores.* Thrift stores often have staplers, file organizers, binders, and other office supplies. I always check there first (especially for cork boards and smaller dry erase boards).

*Facebook Marketplace.* Search for office supplies—or whatever random things you need for your classroom—on Marketplace. You may also post an "in search of" ad for supplies. Often, people have supplies around their home they don't need and are happy to help a teacher out! Sometimes I do a random pen/pencil roundup and ask my Facebook friends nearby to donate all those pens and pencils that are floating randomly around their house.

*Amazon Wishlist.* This is also a great place to let other people know what you need for your classroom. Setting up a wishlist and adding items you need is an easy way to share your needs with parents (and an easy way for them to help you with just a few clicks). Another suggestion: place items of many different price points on your list. Include some low-cost items.

And make sure that everything is eligible for Prime shipping.

---

*A note about Amazon and other wishlists: be mindful of what you request. I've seen teachers request coffee makers and coffee for their classroom. This can be a real turnoff to potential donors, and people reading the list may wonder how essential the rest of the items are. Make sure all of the supplies on the list DIRECTLY benefit your students and are necessities for running your classroom.

---

**Back-to-school sales.** You may not think you need thirty glue sticks in August, but you just might by the time April rolls around. Many stores have back-to-school sales with supplies at their lowest prices of the year. Grab a few extra boxes of markers and pens. This is a great time to add to your class set of rulers and scissors. Keep all of the receipts you get for classroom items and supplies; sometimes you can use these as tax write-offs.

## HOW TO ASK FOR CLASSROOM SUPPLIES

For me, it is always awkward to ask for supply and material donations, but many people want to help. Here are a few groups to hit up:

*Parents.* I always include a link to my Amazon wishlist at parent information nights and at the bottom of newsletters I send to parents. Having an Amazon wishlist is useful because if someone asks to help, you can just direct them to your wishlist and they can decide what they want to donate.

*PTA.* If your school has a PTA, you may want to put in a request for some of the supplies on your list. The PTA is there to support students and teachers, and often they are happy to help with your classroom needs.

*Online donation sites.* There are certain websites designed for teachers to solicit needed classroom supplies and materials. Check out donorschoose.com as a possibility (it is like GoFundMe but specifically for teachers). Sometimes a company or person will sweep through the list and purchase all of the requested items (like when comedian Stephen Colbert bought $800,000 of supplies for South Carolina teachers).[26] Also, many

---

[26] Eric Vilas-Boas, "It's Time for Us to Talk About How Awesome 2015 Was," News, DonorsChoose, December 30, 2015, https://www.donorschoose.org/blog/best-stories-of-2015/.

times corporations will match donations. I have received many items I requested through this site!

## Homework

This homework assignment has two parts.

**PART ONE:**

Create a list of supplies you need. You can write one from scratch, use the suggested list in this chapter, or search for other teacher supply list suggestions. (Expect that you will add to this list as you get settled into your classroom.) Once you have a list, note next to each supply where you will get it. Sometimes your first option won't pan out (maybe the school supply room is empty), but you can at least have an idea of where you will start.

**PART TWO:**

The second assignment for this chapter is  to create a teacher binder. As time goes on and you get into your teaching, you will most likely modify the binder you start out with today, but for now, get a three-ring binder (probably at least one and a half inches wide) and include at least six divider tabs. Include the following tab labels:

- Vision: include your classroom vision developed in chapter 1

- Expectations: include your classroom expectations developed in chapter 2

- Supplies: include your supply list developed in chapter 3

- School Calendars: print out a copy of the school year calendar that lists important dates (first day of school, holidays and vacations, and last day of school). Add this to your binder, as it will help you with long-term planning.

- Contacts: include a list of phone numbers and email addresses for school and district point people. Include the school secretary, principal, and custodian. Although many schools use email as the primary means of communication, it is helpful to also have phone numbers in case of an emergency.

. . . . . . . . . . . . . . . . . . . . . . . . . . . . . . . . . . . . . . .

# Unit 1 Extra Credit

If you are up for a little extra credit, here are a few extra resources to check out:

## SOCIAL MEDIA

Add a few professional "friends" to your social media accounts. Facebook has groups for new teachers where you may feel more open to sharing with other people who are also experiencing this new adventure. When you look for social media accounts to connect with, you may want to find people who teach the same grade level as you. Look for groups with similar interests.

## TWITTER

Two great accounts for educators are @edutopia and @WeAreTeachers.

## WEBSITES

The websites I recommend most to teachers are Cult of Pedagogy by Jennifer Gonzalez (cultofpedagogy.com) and The Cornerstone for Teachers by Angela Watson (thecornerstoneforteachers.com). Both of these sites have something for everyone in many different formats (blogs, podcasts, etc.).

. . . . . . . . . . . . . . . . . . . . . . . . . . . . . . . . . . . . . .

# UNIT 2

---

# Setting Up a Strong Foundation

This unit will start building on the foundation of your classroom vision. You will develop in-depth policies, procedures, plans for building relationships, and plans for communication, and you will begin to identify key support people.

---

# CHAPTER 4

# Procedures and Routines

Procedures and routines will keep your classroom on track and streamline processes so you can focus on teaching. Now that you have your vision and physical classroom setup ready, you can create procedures and routines to guide the everyday workings of the classroom. Go back and find the vision you created. Write it on a sticky note or in the lines below.

## Why Have Procedures and Routines?

Procedures and routines are important for establishing consistency and a way of doing business. Having clearly defined procedures can help your classroom run smoothly so you can spend less time correcting student behavior and more time teaching content. In chapter 2, you created classroom behavior expectations. Now we will drill down to the specific procedures and routines that will give students guidance on how to meet those expectations.

Students find comfort in routines and knowing what is expected of them. While it may seem like a lot of work to create, teach, and practice these routines, it will pay off in the long run. Strongly established procedures guide student behavior and result in less need for redirection or discipline. In a nutshell, procedures and routines can help set the stage for your classroom vision.

---

*What is the difference between a procedure and a routine?* Often, "procedures" and "routines" are grouped together under one umbrella. However, if there were a clear difference between the two, I would suggest that a *routine* is something done regularly by everyone in the class at the same time. For example, there are routines for entering the classroom, passing in papers, or leaving the room at the end of class. A *procedure* is a set of actions used in a specific situation. For example, there is a procedure for how a student finds out what work they missed when they are absent or for how a student should use the hall pass.

---

## When Do You Need
## Procedures and Routines?

There are so many things that happen every day in a classroom. Think back to your time in school. What routines did your teachers establish? Did you stand in a line before entering the classroom in elementary school? Did your teachers expect you to wait to leave the classroom until the bell rang? Were you free to use the hall pass as needed, or was there a way you had to ask permission? When generating a list of everyday events, think through a typical day in your classroom, and then list routines you'd like students to follow for different events throughout the day. Here is a possible list to get you started:

- Entering classroom
- Taking attendance
- Submitting/passing in assignments
- Leaving the class with a hall pass
- Getting materials, supplies, and books during class time
- Putting materials away
- Sharpening pencils
- Writing proper headings on papers (e.g. name, date, class)

- Getting supplies and books
- Working in small groups
- Submitting late or make-up work
- Returning to class after an absence
- Arriving late to class
- Making up missed tests or quizzes

## How to Create Routines and Procedures

Before your students arrive, have your procedures and routines planned out. Students *like* to know what is expected of them, and coming up with procedures on the fly can lead to chaos. There will be situations that come up that you have not planned for. That's okay! Do your best in the moment to guide students through the situation and reflect on it later. If you choose to change how to deal with the situation, that is okay too. The next time you see your students (or before you experience the situation again), give them a heads-up about what you expect from them.

Practice creating routines and procedures. For example, let's look at "entering the room." Think about what you would like students to do as soon as they enter the room at the beginning of class. What will it look and sound like? Would you like them to enter quietly? Do you want them to greet a classmate? Do you want them to immediately grab their materials? Will students do the same thing each day? If they have a warm-up activity, will they know where to find it?

Write down your expectation of what entering the room each day looks like. How will students know what to do? Will you have a note on the board? Will the routine be the same each day, or will it vary?

Here are a few examples:

**ROUTINE:** *Entering the classroom*

What will this look and sound like?

Students will enter the classroom calmly. Some talking is permitted, such as greetings. Students will pick up a half sheet of paper from the table by the door, sit at their seats, and take out their binders. One the half sheet of paper, students will independently answer the warm-up problem posted on the board. After they complete the warm-up problem, students will sit quietly and review notes or assignments from the previous day.

How will the students know what to do?

Routine will be taught at the beginning of the year. A reminder note will be posted in the front of the classroom and on the door as students walk into class.

## PROCEDURE: *Sharpening pencil*

What will this look and sound like?

During instructional time, students will quietly walk to the backup pencil area and take a loaner pencil. During non-instructional time (independent working time), students may quietly walk to the pencil sharpener and sharpen their pencil, then immediately return to their seat. If they borrowed a loaner pencil, they will return the pencil during this time.

How will students know what to do?

Procedure will be shared with students on the first day of school. A small poster will be posted above the pencil sharpener with instructions. A loaner pencil jar will be located next to the pencil sharpener.

## PROCEDURE: *Make-up work for absences*

What will this look and sound like?

Before class starts for the day, students will ask a classmate what they missed during their absence. Students will turn in any work from their time of absence to the "absent" basket located on a specified shelf in the classroom. Students will check the class assignment list for missed assignments, complete missed assignments within two days, and return assignments to the "absent" basket.

How will students know what to do?

I will make a poster for the classroom labeled "I was absent. What do I do?" The poster will give step-by-step instructions on how to ask a classmate what was missed, where to find missed assignments, and where to turn in work.

## PROCEDURE: *Using the hall pass*

What will this look and sound like?

Students will raise their hand and, when called on by the teacher, ask permission to use the hall pass (for example, if the students needs to use the restroom, get water, or get something from their locker or another classroom). When permission is granted, the student will quietly sign the hall pass log located near the door and include their name, the date, and the time they left the room. The student will take the physical hall pass (a clipboard with the room number laminated on it) when they leave the room. Upon their return, the student will return the pass to its spot and write the time of their return on the hall pass log.

How will students know what to do?

Clear instructions for this procedure will be printed and attached to the clipboard and posted next to the hall pass log.

---

*You can create routines for yourself, too. For example, some teachers greet students at the door before class every day. This is a great way to make connections with students, monitor the overall mood, and give students a chance to speak with you if they need to.

## How to Share Routines and Procedures with the Class

Share your routines and procedures within the first week of classes. You may choose to make posters and hang them in the classroom to remind and direct students, or you may print handouts they can keep in their binders. You will need to reiterate the routines frequently at first. Sometimes I remind students each day for the first ten days of school what the hall pass policy is, how to turn in papers, and what is expected of them in terms of classroom behavior.

You will not need to remind students of every procedure every day, though. You may tell the entire class what you expect if they are absent on the first day of school, but then direct them to the instructions posted in the classroom when they need a reminder later. If a student asks what to do after they have been absent, you can direct them to the instructions (and save yourself some time).

It may feel silly, but physically modeling procedures helps students understand the expectations. In my classroom, when students are finished with a test, they turn it into a folder on a table. I literally say, "when you are done testing, please place your test in the folder on the table by the door" as I walk with the folder and set it on the table.

One situation that will likely come up repeatedly over the course of the school year is using the hall pass. Have your procedure clearly thought out ahead of time (Will you have a hall pass that students take with them? Will they sign out? Will you record or limit how often students use the pass? If so, what will you do with this information?). Share this procedure with students on the first day of class, and then share it again each day for the first ten days. I know it sounds like overkill, but many students need to hear this. (Some schools have school-wide hall pass policies, so check with the school before implementing your plan.)

---

*Note for the first day:* I usually start the first day of school by greeting students at the door, telling them their seat assignment, and directing them to read the board for their assignment. Usually the first day's assignment is a short questionnaire and then a quick warm-up to get them thinking about the course content. I try to not spend the entire first day talking about the course syllabus; instead, we do something related to content that also serves as a team-building activity.

---

Don't be alarmed if the first day of school is crazy and tests your flexibility! Have a defined plan for how students will know where to sit and what they will do after they enter, as well as a clear lesson plan for the day. Your plan will most likely need some adjusting on the fly, though. The first day is full of surprises, including students who are late, absent, or in the wrong class. Plan for as much as you can, but be prepared to be flexible.

## Consistency with Routine

After initially sharing your classroom routines and procedures with students, they will need periodic reminders. It is important to be consistent. If for some reason a routine or procedure is changed for a one-time exception, clearly communicate this to your students and explain what the temporary expectation is. If you are not consistent with encouraging and enforcing routines, your students will follow suit, and this may lead to more of your time spent correcting student behavior instead of teaching.

---

*Group work:* The topic of facilitating group work could be an entire college course. There are numerous books, blog posts, articles, and podcasts about how to structure, guide, and grade group work.

When you choose to use group work in your class, read up on how to implement it and find a strategy that works for you. Facilitating group work takes time; you will most likely not be perfect at it the first time, but keep trying. One strategy I always use is to assign group member roles. The entire group is responsible for participating, but one person is the "recorder," one is the "materials manager," one is the "time manager," and one is the "general manager." Be sure to rotate the group roles with each new assignment.

---

*Cellphones/electronic devices*: Before your first class, decide what you will and will not allow in terms of cell phone use. Some teachers have a strict "no cell phone" policy while others allow cell phones for educational purposes or to listen to music during independent work time. If you allow cell phones, you will need to monitor how they are being used, which adds to your to-do list. It may be easier, at least in the beginning of your teaching, to just have a blanket "no cell phone unless explicitly allowed" rule. Some teachers require students to place their cell phones in a specific location (such as a hanging shoe organizer or basket) during class time. Other teachers collect cell phones at the door and redistribute them at the end of class. Find a system that works for you.

## What Happens When Expectations Are Not Followed

In an ideal classroom, your routines and procedures would be clear, all students would follow them, and things would run smoothly. But you will not have the ideal classroom (no teacher does!). Inevitably, students will not always follow your expectations, routines, and procedures, and as the teacher, you will need to correct and redirect student behavior (also known as discipline). When creating a discipline plan, focus on correcting behavior to better align with classroom expectations.

Most discipline plans are based on incremental consequences and lead to stronger action as undesired behavior escalates. For example, not following an expectation may have the following consequences:

1. Gentle reminder (may be given in the form of the "teacher look" or standing near the student and quietly asking them to redirect)

2. Second individual reminder, this time given more sternly

3. Talking to the student outside of class time about behavior

4. Contact parent to discuss behavior

5. Time out in an alternative room (have a teacher nearby who is open to allowing a student to have time out in their classroom)

6. Detention

7. Referral to office

Some teachers choose to post their consequences in the classroom. I usually include them on a syllabus in a condensed style.

1. Reminder

2. Parent email/phone call

3. Detention

4. Referral to office

---

*There are many ways to let students know you disapprove of their behavior. One way is the "teacher look," a stern and almost emotionless look directed at a student participating in undesirable behavior. Another way to communicate to a student can be through a hand signal. For example, if you hold your pointer finger up while looking at a student, you are letting them know you see their behavior and they need to change it.

---

When outlining discipline steps with students, I try to stay as general as possible and allow myself the flexibility to add other steps in between. I share the condensed list of four consequences, but in my mind, I know I will use the list of seven (I just don't share this with the students). In the classroom, student misbehavior can be distracting and throw you off your teacher game, so have your thorough list of disciplinary steps ready (perhaps printed and easily referenceable) for you to use in the moment.

---

*Keeping Records:* You may find that you have a few students who require a lot of your disciplinary attention. Be sure to take note of every disciplinary intervention you use. If I were using the disciplinary consequences listed 1–7, I would keep a record each time I made contact home or any subsequent, more serious consequence. If you notice that some students need frequent reminders, begin to note how often this happens. If you find a pattern, you may want to call home. Whether it is a phone call home or a referral to the principal you will need to have (and will be glad to have) records.

---

## Homework

Generate a set of routines and procedures and a firm discipline plan. If you have not yet clearly laid out all of your routines and procedures, pick two or three to write up. Then list other situations that will require a routine or procedure. Create a clear, incremental discipline plan too. Write this up and print it out. Create two plans: one for you and a shorter, more concise list to share with students.

Print your routines and procedures and your discipline plan and add it to the teacher binder you started in the chapter 3 homework.

# CHAPTER 5

# Relationship Building and Communication with Students and Parents

Now that your class vision, procedures, and discipline plan have been established, this chapter will guide you through building relationships. Relationships are vital to education,[27] and establishing relationships with students and parents will build a strong foundation for learning in your classroom.

---

[27] Sarah D. Sparks, "Why Teacher-Student Relationships Matter," Education Week, March 12, 2019, https://www.edweek.org/ew/articles/2019/03/13/why-teacher-student-relationships-matter.html.

## Why Student-Teacher and Parent-Teacher Relationships Are Important

Learning cannot happen when the student is stressed or feels emotionally unsafe. In order to build a trusting environment, it is vital to form relationships with students. A student-teacher relationship is not like a regular friendship; it is more of a mentoring relationship. Teachers should be socially engaging with their students, but they must also connect with students on a deeper level. Understanding students' interests, strengths, and habits allows teachers to be more effective.[28]

In addition to building relationships with your students, it is also important to build relationships with their parents. Positive teacher-parent relationships have been shown to improve student academic achievement and support student social and emotional well-being.[29] While relationships with parents will likely not be as intense or deep as those with your students, opening that line of communication can help students achieve more.

---

[28] Ibid.

[29] Susan M. Sheridan, Ph.D., "Establishing healthy parent-teacher relationships for early learning success," Early Learning Network, August 29, 2018, http://earlylearningnetwork.unl.edu/2018/08/29/parent-teacher-relationships/.

*Sending out regular and concise information to parents can open the lines of communication.

*When I use the term "parent," I mean the adult(s) who act(s) as a student's primary caregiver or guardian (maybe a grandparent, uncle or aunt, or foster parent).

## How to Build Student-Teacher and Parent-Teacher Relationships

It will take time to build relationships with your students. The beginning of the school year can be especially over-whelming with learning the lay of the land, getting into the rhythm of the school day, lesson planning, paperwork, and more . . . but even with all of that going on, it's still worthwhile to take time to connect with students each day. Most teachers say that the best part of teaching is working with students. Building those relationships will not only benefit your students, but it will have a positive impact on you too! Often, my students are the ones who give me the energy to keep showing up!

I find that there are a few musts for building relationships (which will in turn build trust, which will in turn yield greater learning). First, learn how to pronounce each student's name, and if they prefer a nickname, use that. Second, touch base with each student every day. That can mean greeting each student at the door or walking through the classroom and saying a personal hello to everyone. Third, find something you and the student have in common (it can be something as simple as "we both have a brother"). There are tons of "getting to know you" forms for students that you can find with a Google search.

Give yourself time to learn about your students. For the first few weeks, spend a few minutes each day talking to them as a group or individually. Some teachers love "ice breaker" activities, but some don't. Find what works for you and what you feel comfortable with. Once you find something you can talk about with each student, make a note of it in your binder. Check in with the student on the topic randomly. If a student is involved in an extracurricular activity such as drama or a sport, go and watch them perform or play if you have the time. The time you spend making connections and showing you care will pay off in the long run.

When you have a large number of students, remembering all of their likes, hobbies, and activities can be difficult (especially when you are just meeting the students). If you give a survey to students at the beginning of the year, you can always refer back to it once you get to know your students. A good time to remind yourself of their interests is October, after school has been in session for a while and everyone in the classroom is more comfortable with each other.

---

*One relationship-building strategy I like is a modified version of "Two Truths and a Lie." For this activity, I assign students into groups of four or fewer. The groups come up with two things that are true about all the people in the group and one thing that is a lie about all of the group members. For example, a group could list, "we all like math, we all have a brother, and we all skateboard." The groups then share their lists with the rest of the class, and everyone tries to figure out which statement is the lie. This will help you learn more about your students, but it will also help your students find commonalities among themselves. I often use this activity the first time I put students into groups.

---

## Communication

Strong relationships are built on clear and consistent communication. Both parents and students should know what to expect in terms of when and how you will communicate with them.

### WHAT NEEDS TO BE COMMUNICATED

Think about what you will need to include in communications to students and parents. One way to do this is to generate a list of questions you predict students and parents will ask. Here are a few examples:

- What are the behavior expectations?
- What is the homework?
- How do I check my grade?
- How do I figure out what I missed if I'm absent?
- When will the next test be?
- What is the best way to reach you (email, phone, etc.)?

### HOW TO COMMUNICATE

For each question you come up with, think of how you will communicate the answer. For example, will homework always be posted in one place on a white-board in the room? Will it also be posted online? Will you have a calendar with upcoming test dates posted in the room? Once you have decided how you will communicate information, make sure to share this with students and parents at the beginning of the school year.

There are many ways to share important information with students and parents. Weekly or monthly agendas can be posted on a whiteboard in the classroom and also emailed to students and parents. One teacher writes important upcoming dates on the whiteboard at the beginning of a unit of study, then snaps a picture of the dates on her phone and sends an email out to parents and students. My elementary teacher colleagues often use weekly newsletters to share information with parents. In a regular newsletter, you can let parents know about upcoming tests, projects, and other work. You can also include reminders of where to check grades or make up work after an absence.

---

*all important messages to students need to be shared verbally *and* visually. Don't just verbally announce when an upcoming test will be: also keep it posted on the board.

---

## HARD CONVERSATIONS WITH PARENTS

Some conversations with parents will be difficult to have. It can be uncomfortable to talk about a student's poor academic performance, behavior issues, or other concerns. Some parents will be supportive of you while others may be defensive of their children (and themselves). Remind the parent that you are coming from a place of caring and concern. You may want to open your conversation with just that—you are reaching out with concerns and would like to help the parent support their child.

## BACK-TO-SCHOOL NIGHT

Back-to-school night is a common event at most schools. It usually happens within the first month of the school year. Typically, the format is that parents travel through their children's school schedule to meet their teachers. If the student has multiple teachers, each mock "class period" is about ten minutes. Use this time to communicate the following:

- A little about your background (where you attended college, a few of your hobbies, etc.)
- Your teaching philosophy (maybe even include your classroom vision)

- A quick rundown of the course (standards, major projects, how grades will be determined)
- The best way to communicate with you
- Ways parents can help (this is a great place to share your classroom supply wishlist)

Be ready to answer common questions:

- Is there extra credit?
- Is there homework?
- What percent of the grade do tests account for?
- How can parents find out what the assignments are and when tests will be?

---

*If you have already thought through these questions, you may want to make a "Frequently Asked Questions" handout with answers provided.

---

**85**

Stress to parents that the evening event is to cover class basics, and if they have specific questions about their child, you will be happy to answer those questions another time. Make sure your contact information is readily available. Parents who want to talk about their children can reach out to you to set up a time to talk. One way I politely defer parent conferences during back-to-school night is by saying something like, "I would be happy to talk to you about your student, but right now I can't give you my full attention. Will you please email me so we can set up a time to chat?"

Plan your presentation and do a few practice runs before the event. I usually have a PowerPoint or Google Slide presentation ready and copies of the syllabus/course policies printed out. Sometimes, if I have time to stop at a store, I pick up cookies to serve as parents walk in.

## PRACTICE TALKING TO PARENTS

Talking to parents can be intimidating, especially if this is your first teaching job or if you don't have children of your own. I remember being twenty-two years old and having parents ask me how they should parent their children. I did not know how to respond. I was shocked the first time I called a parent and the parent questioned my account of their child's behavior. Since then, I have developed a little thicker skin and have learned to keep conversations evidence-based and focused on the student.

If you need to have a conversation about student misbehavior, paint a clear picture of what the problem is, evidence of the problem, and an idea for a possible solution. I usually provide a suggestion for a solution and then ask the parent if they can support me or if they have any other ideas. (This is also a time when keeping records of student behavior comes in handy.)

Anticipate what your conversation with a parent will be like. You may want to use another teacher, your spouse, a friend, or an administrator to practice conversations before contacting parents. Running it through with another person may bring up other questions the parent could ask, and you will be prepared to answer. As in the classroom, if a parent asks you a question you do not know the answer to, you can respond, "I would like some time to think about that. I will respond by tomorrow through email," or something along those lines. If you feel that the conversation with the parent may turn hostile, invite the principal, the school counselor, your department head, or other administrator to attend the conference with you.

## Homework

Plan how to build relationships with students and parents. List three ways you can find out more about your students and two things you can do to proactively connect with students. Make a list of topics you will need to communicate about and how you will share this information.

# CHAPTER 6

# The Important People (Your Life Lines)

The previous chapter focused on developing relationships with your students and their parents. This chapter will focus on developing relationships with your colleagues and creating a plan of where to go when you need support or have a question. You will develop a plan for building teacher/teacher, teacher/administrator, and teacher/staff relationships.

## Relationships with Colleagues

Teaching can be a lonely job. Often, you are the only adult in the room for hours on end. To help keep your sanity and morale up, create a professional support system. You may have a mentor, be part of a professional learning community with other teachers at your school, find a supportive administrator, or reach out to other places such as conferences, social media, or bloggers. It will probably be a combination of all the above.

> "It's so important to have relationships with colleagues who you can run ideas by, talk to about your day, and bond with. Teaching is tough! We need each other. That said, avoid the ones who drain your energy."
>
> —LAURIE H.

> "My colleagues support, encourage, and share ideas with me.  It is through these interactions that I start to see things from a different perspective and consider opinions formerly unknown, all in the name of personal and group development."
>
> —KELLY M.

## Mentors

Mentoring programs can provide you with emotional and instructional support. They have been found to increase the likelihood of new teachers staying in teaching.[30] One of the most important people I recommend you connect with is a mentor.

New teachers are often assigned a mentor through an induction program, through their school district, or at their site. If you are assigned an official mentor, reach out to establish a relationship (more on that shortly). If you are not assigned an official mentor and you had a teacher mentor before that you respect, ask if they will continue to foster your development as a teacher. When you ask a mentor to continue with you, be sure to mention that you have learned so much from them and that you would like to keep the relationship going. Ask if they are willing to help with questions you have as the school year progresses.

If you are not assigned a mentor and have not had one in the past (or if you had one in the past and are ready for a new experience), seek one out. Ideally, you will be able to find a mentor at your school. Don't limit your search to only teachers who teach the same grade or

---

[30] Linda Darling-Hammond, "Keeping Good Teachers: Why It Matters, What Leaders Can Do," Educational Leadership, May 2003, http://www. ascd.org/publications/educational-leadership/may03/vol60/num08/ Keeping-Good-Teachers@-Why-It-Matters,-What-Leaders-Can-Do. aspx.

subject as you; sometimes you can learn a lot more about the practice of teaching when you learn from someone who teaches different content.

It may take a few weeks into the school year to find a mentor. One strategy for identifying a mentor is to listen to what your students say. Do they talk about how much they learn from or respect a particular teacher? If so, reach out and ask that person if you can talk to them about their teaching practice. Even better, ask other teachers if you can observe them teaching. Seeing other teachers in action is a great way to learn new teaching moves.

When you have identified a potential mentor, it can be intimidating to reach out to them. Consider sending an email introducing yourself (include a few of your hobbies and why you chose to go into teaching), describing what you are looking for in a mentor relationship (such as advice on lesson planning and classroom management), and explaining why you asked this particular person (the qualities they have that you think would help you grow as a teacher).

Once you have established a mentor, set a few boundaries for your relationship (more about boundaries in a few chapters). Here are a few things to consider talking about at the beginning of your relationship:

- How will you communicate?
- How often will you meet?
- Will you meet face to face? Through email? Virtual meetings?
- Will your meetings be scheduled or as needed?
- What type of feedback do you want from your mentor?
- How much time does your mentor have to dedicate to you?

**\*KEEP IN MIND:**

- Most mentors mentor you because they truly believe in you and your potential!
- Most mentors aren't paid (or their stipend is pennies on the hour). They are not in it for the money; they are in it for you and your current and future students.
- Mentors want you to succeed!
- Mentors are learners too. They won't have all the answers, but they will probably have some ideas.

- Most mentors want to learn from you too!

- If your relationship is not working, find another mentor. Your mentor relationship should make you feel valued, respected, and supported.

## Collaborating with Colleagues

You will most likely be working in collaborative groups (sometimes called PLCs, Professional Learning Communities, teams, departments . . . whatever the buzzword is that year). This is a great place to find support, but you must also be a little cautious. Often, these types of groups are assigned and you will have no choice about whom you work with. Sometimes these groups can get a little callous.

Whatever the circumstances of your collaboration assignment, expect to learn something from your groupmates. As a new teacher, be open to what more experienced teachers think, but remain true to your teaching philosophy (do remember, though, that your philosophy will probably change over time).

As a new teacher, I suggest you do a lot of listening and thinking during the first few meetings with a new group. Hear what the other teachers are saying and reflect on how it aligns with your practice. In time, offer suggestions and opinions. In my experience, veteran teachers are more willing to listen to someone who has been part of the group for a while rather than someone who is brand new to both teaching and the group. Be like a sponge. Absorb everything you see and hear from other teachers, then keep what works for you and reject what doesn't.

---

*You will likely be collaborating with other teachers, either in groups or as a pair. As a new teacher, you have a fresh perspective and will have learned the latest teaching practices in your credential program. New teachers are a great asset to collaboration groups. However, sometimes veteran teachers may not be excited about revamping their curriculum or teaching methods. Tread lightly when working with other teachers; share your new ideas, but remain open to what other teachers have learned from their experience.

---

*Sometimes there will be groups of teachers who are constantly negative. While venting frustrations is okay, steer away from people who only focus on the negative, don't try to come up with solutions, and aren't open to change. Surround yourself with realistic and positive people. This will help keep your mood up and give you a positive, supportive place to go when you need encouragement.

## Other School Staff

In addition to other teachers, there will be school staff members who can provide support. If there is an administrator you feel comfortable with, use them as a resource. Sometimes teachers feel uneasy about confiding in administrators because administrators are also their evaluators. This can pose a tricky situation . . . you want to come to someone with questions and to share your thinking, but you may be concerned that they will use your lack of experience to negatively evaluate you. Find someone you can trust; you may want to talk to other teachers to scout out an administrator who will be supportive. For example, if you want to try out a new technology in your class, ask around to see which administrator is encouraging of technology and can help get you set up. Finding ideas you have in common with administrators can lead to a relationship where you can go for extra support. Librarians and other school technology and instructional specialists can also be of great support to you. Many school librarians and support staffers can help with ideas for lesson planning and finding resources, and some will even teach or co-teach lessons.

## Support Outside of School

Mentors, fellow teachers, and staff members can provide you with in-person and daily support, but there are many other places to find support. Social media is a great place to find teaching inspiration and help. Educators are all over Instagram, Twitter, and Pinterest. Search hashtags related to your subject area, or even try searching #new-teacher. Engage in Twitter chats, even if you mostly just read. (I often follow chats, and when I find a comment that resonates with me, I follow the person who commented or look at their bio to see if they have a website or blog.) People on social media *want* to be social. If you see something that you are interested in trying out, reach out to the author and ask for ideas on implementing it.

When using social media, though, it's a good idea to

make a separate professional account for your work. That way, you can build a teaching community without exposing your personal life. When connecting professionally on social media, stick to education and teaching. Sharing what you ate for lunch (unless it was a school lunch) or a crazy picture of you out with friends may not make for the best professional image.

In addition to being another means of support, people outside of your immediate campus can provide different viewpoints. If you teach in an urban school, someone from a rural school may have an idea you never would have thought of on your own. You may also see and hear viewpoints you don't agree with or that challenge your philosophies. This can help you grow as an educator and change your educational ideas (or confirm your current practice).

## Homework

Identify current or possible support people. In chapter 2, you identified key staff members; now, identify key faculty and other staff members you can turn to. Next, include your current mentor's contact information in your teacher binder, or create a list of possible mentors. Jot down a list of questions that you can ask a mentor.

. . . . . . . . . . . . . . . . . . . . . . . . . . . . . . . . . . . . .

# UNIT 2 EXTRA CREDIT

Whether you are assigned a mentor or seek one out on your own, identify other inspirational educators. Places to go to find inspiration include social media, blogs, bookstores (Education sections), or speakers at conferences and workshops. Find someone (or a few people) with similar educational philosophies and "friend" or "follow" them.

. . . . . . . . . . . . . . . . . . . . . . . . . . . . . . . . . . . . .

# UNIT 3

---

# The Daily Grind–Lesson Planning, Grading, and Record Keeping

This unit will get down and dirty and dive into the hard part of teaching . . . the day-to-day grind. This unit's goal is to provide you with a game plan to sustain yourself through the hard parts of teaching and give you strategies for immediate and long-term success!

This unit will focus on lesson planning, grading, and the daily administrative and paperwork tasks you will have to accomplish. You'll find ideas for how to set up systems and streamline your processes to focus on your teaching and prevent burnout.

# CHAPTER 7

# Lesson Planning

Something you will learn early on (if you haven't already) is that in teaching you will never have enough time to finish everything that you want to finish. I remember my first few years when I would work hours past the last bell and go home thinking I could stay all night and still not be caught up. This is the nature of teaching, and after twenty years, I still could fill all of my days with teaching tasks. But outrageous hours in "teacher mode" will most likely lead you to burnout. Yes, your first few years you will be working more hours than the veteran teachers because it takes time to learn the ropes, but you must also put boundaries around your time (more about this in a few chapters). This chapter will focus on creating systems around lesson planning.

## Lesson Planning

Detailed lesson planning was probably included in your teacher credentialing program, and throughout your teacher training, you were most likely required to write up official lesson plans. These lessons are often very detailed and highly scripted. The practice of creating detailed lesson plans is great for learning the intricacies of teaching and lesson design; however, it is not sustainable to create meticulously detailed lesson plans for every lesson, every day.

Keep in mind that lesson planning is a very personal process. Some teachers make very detailed plans for each day, some have a skeleton outline, and some plan in their head on their drive to work in the morning. For your first few years, I suggest you find a happy medium. You want to have a clear road map of where you want your students to go in the curriculum, but you don't want to spend so much time on tiny details every day that you burn yourself out.

The first step is to create a large overview. Traditionally, these larger views are called "units," and within each unit are smaller "lessons." I used a lesson planning strategy as I planned and wrote this guidebook. I first thought about the overall goal of the book: "give teachers a clear roadmap on how to focus their teaching ideas into a vision for their classrooms, and then develop a structured plan for how to create and maintain that vision." I then developed this book with a clear learning goal for each chapter, so each chapter is a smaller lesson. The two questions I always ask when planning a lesson are, "What do I want my students to know and be able to do by the end of this lesson?" and "How will I know they have mastered the concept?" Though these questions seem straightforward, many teachers have difficulty answering them. Let's break it down.

## Units
## (Creating Overall Views of Learning)

When looking at a unit of study, you want to get the overall idea of what students will learn. I think of a unit as a collection of lessons that all lead to a bigger picture or understanding. Here is an example from a math unit:

> Fractions: Students will understand what a fractional number is and how to apply the four arithmetic operations (addition, subtraction, multiplication, and division) arithmetically.

When developing a unit, make sure it is broad, but also describes what you want students to do. When I develop a unit goal, I think beyond a single "thing." In math, if the unit was just labeled as the "thing," then "fractions" would be too broad. What do you want students to understand and be able to do with fractions?

---

*When creating a unit goal, it is better to be more specific than less specific. As you develop the lessons within the unit, you can always go back and make a more generalized description of the unit.

---

To determine what a unit is and how much understanding it will cover, a good frame of reference is the textbook (if you are using one), district- or school-developed courses of study, or, if your course has standards, grouping standards into like categories. Also, think about what an assessment would entail. Is the unit large enough to create a culminating assessment that allows students to demonstrate their mastery of the unit?

---

*When talking about creating units based on the test, I do not mean that you should "teach to the test." However, creating a test before planning the lessons in the unit can help guide you as you create lessons. Many teachers use this strategy, called "backward planning." They look at the end goal of the unit, create an assessment, then break the unit down into lessons. More about assessments in the next chapter!

---

*In English, one of my pet peeves is when a unit is labeled by the title of the book the class is using. When teachers say, "I am teaching *Othello*," it does not describe exactly what they are teaching. In this case, the teacher is using *Othello* to teach some concepts and skills, so title the unit with that.

---

## Lessons

When developing lessons, I suggest breaking the unit goal down into smaller and more detailed pieces. Using the math example:

Fractions: Students will understand what a fractional number is and how to apply the four arithmetic operations (addition, subtraction, multiplication, and division) arithmetically.

I may decide to break the unit down into the six lessons:

- What a fraction represents, how to represent it in multiple ways (percents, decimals), and where a fraction is on a number line
- Adding fractions
- Subtracting fractions
- Multiplying fractions
- Dividing fractions
- Simplifying expressions involving fractions

Next, I will plan each lesson by asking myself, "What do I want my students to know and be able to do?" and "How will I know they have mastered the concept?"

## WHAT DO I WANT MY STUDENTS TO KNOW AND BE ABLE TO DO?

Though this question seems easy to answer, it may give

you a headache. For each lesson, first drill down to what it is you want students to know. For example, in the fraction unit, I may choose this lesson: "Students know what a fraction represents, how to represent it in multiple ways (percents, decimals), and where a fraction is on a number line." Now that I know what I want my students to know, I need to create a statement about what they can do. My statement may be, "Students will be able to describe what a fraction is. When given a fractional number, they will be able to write the equivalent percent and decimal representation. They will be able to place a fractional number on the number line, and they will be able to identify a fractional number that is represented on a number line." Notice these ideas are still general. I have not mentioned any specific fractional numbers yet.

---

*Some teachers write these "what do I want my students to know and be able to do?" ideas in the form of learning targets or other "I can" statements. If your school requires you write learning targets in student-friendly language, this is a great time in your lesson development to create those targets.

---

## HOW WILL I KNOW MY STUDENTS HAVE MASTERED THE CONCEPT?

This is where you want to get specific. Using the same lesson as above, I will develop criteria for what students will produce and share with me that shows their mastery.

| KNOW AND BE ABLE TO DO | HOW THEY WILL SHOW MASTERY (SPECIFIC EXAMPLE) |
|---|---|
| Students will be able to describe what a fraction is. | Students will use words to define what a fraction is (for example, "a fraction is a number that represents parts of a whole"). |
| Given a fractional number, students will be able to write the equivalent percent and decimal representation. | Given the fraction 3/8, students will be able to write the equivalent percent (37.5%) and the equivalent decimal (.375). |
| Students will be able to place a fractional number on the number line. | Given the fraction 3/8 and a number line labeled with integers, students will be able to plot the number 3/8. |
| Students will be able to identify a fractional number that is represented on a number line. | Given a number line labeled with integers and a plot at 7/4, students will be able to identify the plot as 7/4. |

*Note:* this lesson can be modified for different grade levels. For example, I could limit the fractional numbers to 1/2s, or only use like fractions when adding and subtracting.

## LEARNING ACTIVITIES

The learning activities are often the most fun for teachers to plan. I mean, it is the heart of teaching . . . what you are *actually* going to do to help students learn the concepts. This is where you can do a lecture, have students do guided research, or have students perform and experiment. The world is your oyster on this. I won't spend a lot of time talking about learning activities, as the types of activities will vary based on grade level, subject area, and teacher preference. I'd rather focus on creating really good lesson goals, which is applicable to you no matter what subject or grade level you teach. If you need more ideas for activities, talk to a subject-alike teacher.

*A mentor teacher is a great resource for learning activities. They can guide you on what has worked and what has flopped in their classroom.

## FORMATIVE ASSESSMENTS

Formative assessments are ways of checking for understanding throughout a lesson and unit. More on formative assessments will be discussed in the next chapter. For now, if you don't know what formative assessments you will use, revisit this lesson plan in the next chapter.

## SUPPORT FOR ALL STUDENTS

Support for all students includes teaching moves and learning aids you will provide so all students can access the material. You know your students best. Some have official, designated supports (such as Individual Education Plans/IEPs or supports for English language learners), while some students may not have official support requirements, but as their teacher, you know them and are able to provide scaffolds to make learning accessible. Some ideas for supports may include:

- A handout copy of notes (either filled in or left blank for students to fill in)
- Subtitles captioned when playing video
- Mathematical manipulatives (such as blocks or an abacus)

- Repeating instructions verbally three times and writing instructions on the board
- Having a multilingual glossary for key words used in the lesson

## PRACTICE ACTIVITIES

"Practice activities" have many names. They are sometimes called "individual practice" or "homework." Practice activities include anything that students do to practice the skills from the lesson. This will look different in different subject areas.

## UNIT PLAN TEMPLATE

| UNIT PLAN | NAME OF UNIT: |
|---|---|
| Goals: | |
| Topics: | |
| | |
| | |
| | |
| | |
| | |
| | |
| | |

# LESSON PLAN TEMPLATE

| Name of Lesson: |  |
| --- | --- |

| Standards (if applicable): |  |
| --- | --- |

| What do I want my students to know and be able to do? | How will I know they have mastered the concept? |
| --- | --- |

| Learning Activities: |  |
| --- | --- |

| Formative Assessment to include in the lesson: | Supports for all students to include in lesson: |
| --- | --- |

| Practice Activities: |  |
| --- | --- |

*If your school requires you have learning
  objectives on the board each day, you
  can use the unit goal or each lesson goal.
  You can also share these with students,
  which will allow them to self-assess their
  understanding.

You will need to be flexible when teaching . . . sometimes your lessons won't go as planned. Be ready to adjust based on student feedback and understanding. I want to point out that your lesson plan serves as your roadmap toward a final destination. Sometimes you will change your route while you're in progress, and that is totally okay! Just make sure that you and your students get to your final destination.

*Teaching Tip:* On Friday, make sure you
  have everything prepared (papers printed,
  learning targets, etc.) for Monday.

## Homework

Create a unit plan and a lesson plan (use a lesson that will be included in the unit plan). If the templates in this chapter work for you, use those. If not, identify a template you have used before that you like or find a different one to try on the internet.

Alternate assignment: If you do not have a current teaching position, you can still practice the concepts from this chapter. Using a lesson plan developed in your teacher preparation program, see if you can make it even better using ideas from this chapter.

# CHAPTER 8

---

# Assessment and Grading

Assessment and grading are very touchy subjects in the teaching community. You will find that there as many perspectives as there are teachers. Unless you are mandated by your school to assess or grade a certain way, most teachers determine their own way of doing these things. I do not want to tell you how to assess or grade, although I do have some opinions about it (send me an email and I'll share!), but I want to offer some things to think about regarding assessment. Because grading and assessment go hand in hand (oftent, grades are determined by student assessments), this chapter will look at both topics. First, we will look at assessments, and then we will move to grading. Hopefully, the assessment piece will give you some ideas on how to incorporate student assessment into a course grade.

## Two Types of Assessments

There are two types of assessments: formative assessment and summative assessment. *Formative assessments* are meant to inform you and the student of the student's progress toward mastery. Many times, formative assessments are referred to as "assessment *for* learning." *Summative assessments* usually occur at the end of a unit (or sometimes at the end of a lesson) and help teachers determine if the student learned what they set out to teach. Summative assessment is often referred to as "assessment *of* learning." We'll dive into each in a little more detail next.

## Formative Assessment

Throughout your teaching, you should be monitoring students' learning. There are many ways to do this, and these are known as formative assessments. Based on your feedback from formative assessments, you can change your lesson to reteach or reinforce certain concepts, or perhaps skip over part of a lesson if students demonstrate advanced understanding. The key to formative assessment is that students and teachers can use it to gauge student understanding. Students should be aware of what you are doing and why you are doing it so they can reflect on their own learning.

In classrooms, I hear teachers and students label quizzes as formative assessments. These are a great example, especially if the teacher uses feedback from the quizzes to tweak their instruction. For example, if you give a quiz and everyone bombs one of the questions, that is a topic or skill you know you will need to go back and review again. It is especially helpful if you give students feedback on quizzes instead of just marking an item wrong. There are many ways to provide feedback on quizzes. You can handwrite notes to each student prompting them to thinking about the questions, or you can have students look at each other's quizzes and, with your guidance, review and give feedback.

---

*A strategy I saw in one of my colleague's classrooms was a "key" posted on the board. He would use a letter or symbol to provide feedback on students' papers, and the students would use the key to decode what his comment was. For example, "d" meant "add more detail here," "w" meant "I can't understand what you wrote here," "i" meant "this does not follow the instructions," and so on. You can review a paper and place multiple letters or symbols throughout.

---

Other, often more subtle, methods of formative assessment include any way you gather data on students' current understanding. There are hundreds of ways of collecting evidence of student learning. These are a few methods of formative assessment to get you thinking:

- **Individual whiteboards:** ask students a question and have them write their answer on a personal whiteboard and hold it up. The teacher can scan the room quickly to get a sense of understanding.

- **Online apps:** there are many programs that serve as a "virtual whiteboard." Students can use their phones or other technology to respond to a prompt and the teacher sees the results.

- **Show on fingers:** there are many ways students can use their hands to convey understanding. One strategy is to ask students how comfortable they are with the material on a scale of one to five (one being "totally confused" and five being "I could teach this"). You could also pose multiple-choice questions and have students show their answers with their fingers (one finger raised is A, two fingers is B, three fingers is C, four fingers is D, and five fingers is E). Students can hold their hands up to their chests to confidentially share their answers without feeling pressure (or without being able to copy another student's answer).

• **Peer feedback:** this is especially meaningful with older students. Students exchange papers and then give feedback to other students using a rubric or other model answer. There are many protocols for this type of feedback, and students will most likely need training on how to give their peers feedback.

- **Exit slips:** these are traditionally used at the end of class. Pose students a question and have them answer it and submit on their way out of class. This is great for gathering feedback and preparing for the next class. You can also use these slips in the middle of a lesson. Students can answer a question or demonstrate their understanding quickly, and you can quickly go through the stack and see how students are doing. This can also be done electronically.

The key to formative assessments is that students are also in on it. They are able to use the assessment to monitor their progress toward the learning goal. This part of the process is essential, and when you use formative assessments, encourage students to also notice how they respond.

*Thinking about your thinking:*
metacognition is a great skill for any
student have throughout life. Formative
assessment is a process that allows for
this. Being explicit about students using
formative assessment can help them
practice this type of reflective thinking.

## SUMMATIVE ASSESSMENT

Summative assessments are typically given at the end
of a unit. They summarize the student's mastery of the
subject. Summative assessments come in many forms,
including unit tests, projects, essays, and final exams.

If you create your summative assessment before
teaching a unit, it will guide your instruction. After you
have created the unit goal (see the previous chapter) and
have settled on the topics within that unit, make a summative assessment. This is a step that many teachers do
not do (I will admit, it is not something I have always
done), but when I do, it makes my lesson planning a lot
smoother. It also makes the end of a unit, when I typically
review, a lot easier because I know exactly what students
will need to do.

*When you create a summative assessment as you develop a unit plan, don't be afraid to tweak the assessment as you teach. You may discover that the way you thought you would want students to demonstrate their understanding will not give you the information you need. Figure this out during individual lessons and revamp your summative test or project as you go.

Because a summative assessment is an assessment of learning, this data is often used to report a student's understanding of the material. Unlike a formative assessment, a summative assessment is typically done at the end of a lesson, which means that teachers may not have the time to reteach concepts that were missed. Teachers usually use summative assessments to reflect most of (or at least part of) a student's grade. You will need to determine what works for you.

## Grading

There are numerous books and courses on assessment and grading. Some people have built their entire careers around studying and sharing ideas about these topics.

Grading is an especially personal topic for teachers—so sensitive, in fact, that I have witnessed some very heated discussions about the topic between teachers. You will ultimately have to determine your own grading policies (unless you are at a school that has grading mandates). This section cannot cover every intricacy, but it will give you a good start and a solid plan for you to take to your classroom. Here are some items to consider as you develop your grading policy for your class.

First, think about what you want a grade to reflect. Do you want it to be mastery of the subject? Do you want it to reflect effort? Do you want it to be a combination of both?

Next, think about how you will determine grades. Will you look at both formative and summative assessments? Will they have equal weight? What about classroom participation? How much will you include effort into the grade? Will the class include homework? If so, how much of the grade will you value on homework? Will you grade homework for completion or correctness? However you decide to determine grades, be sure to share with students how they will be graded early in the course.

*You don't have to attach a grade to everything students do. Sometimes practice can be just that—practice—without an official grade attached.

Sometimes an easy way to break down grades is by percentages. What percentage will you assign to effort, and what percentage will you assign to assessment? (When I say "effort," I mean work that is done for completion, not necessarily correctness.) You can also include a category for class participation and behavior. I try to keep grading percentages simple; for example, 90% assessment (graded for correctness) and 10% assignments (graded for effort). I also include a clause that says these are approximate and can change. Having broad categories allows you to adjust your instruction, adding assessments and assignments as needed.

---

*Some schools and content departments have agreed-upon grade percentage breakdowns. Check with your department as you make your grading plan.

---

Whatever you decide to include in the grade, be sure to determine how you will record it. Assessment and assignment grades are an easy entry into the grade book, but if you decide to include class participation and behavior in the course grade, decide early how you will determine this part of the grade.

## HOT TOPICS

When it comes to assessment and grading, some topics are discussed frequently in education circles and are worth considering for your own class:

- **Test or assessment retakes.** Will you allow students to retake assessments? If so, will there be criteria in place (for example, they must show they did extra practice problems or made test corrections before retaking the assessment)? How will you grade the retake and determine the score for your grade book?

- **Formative Assessments.** Will you enter formative assessment grades in the grade book? Which types of formative assessments, such as quizzes, will be included in a student's grade? If a student shows improvement (for example, a student fails a quiz but then shows proficiency on the unit assessment), will you raise the original grade?

- **Alternative ways of showing mastery.** What will you do if a student "isn't a good test taker" or prefers an alternative form of assessment? Will you create these yourself or allow students to create them? Will you accept alternative forms of showing mastery?

## Homework

For this chapter's homework, there are two assignments.

First, go back to the lesson plan you developed in the previous chapter and add formative strategies you plan to use.

Second, determine how you will decide student grades. Put together a grading policy for your course. Add this grading system to your teacher binder.

# CHAPTER 9

# Staying Organized and Managing Paperwork

Now that you are well underway with your plans for your classroom, keeping the plan on track by setting up organizational systems is key. This chapter will focus on strategies for how to organize materials, lesson plans, communication records, and disciplinary action records. While this chapter will provide you with a list of things that you need to organize and suggestions for how to do that, organization is a very personal topic and you will need to find what works best for you.

## Lesson Plans

You will most likely teach the same subject and courses in consecutive years, especially if you stay at the same school. You'll want to have an organization system for your lesson plans so you can refer back to them in future years (this is one reason teaching gets easier with time—you have done some of the heavy lifting in previous years). How you decide to organize and archive these lessons is up to you. Some teachers like to keep their lessons electronically or digitally, some keep their lesson plans on a calendar, some keep their lesson plans filed in a binder, and I've even seen some teachers file lesson plans in manila folders by unit chapter.

There are two types of lesson plans that you will want to keep organized so you can refer to them during the current school year and in future school years: long-term plans and daily lessons.

## LONG-TERM PLANS

Your long-term plans include a course pacing overview for units. As you design your school year curriculum, you will want to chunk out time slots for your units so you can stay on pace. These long-term plans do not have to include individual lessons, but rather overviews (think about the units we described in chapter 7). You may want to add how many days of instruction each unit will require; this will allow you to compare your unit plans with a calendar and pace them out. You can use monthly calendars, yearly calendars, or a customized calendar. Here is an example of a unit paced on a monthly calendar:

| SUNDAY | MONDAY | TUESDAY | WEDNESDAY | THURSDAY | FRIDAY | SATURDAY |
|---|---|---|---|---|---|---|
| | | | 1 | 2 | 3 | 4 |
| 5 | 6<br>NO SCHOOL | 7<br>Dog Park 2<br>Unit 4 | 8<br>How Much Can it Hold? | 9<br>What Do You See? And Ready, Set, Draw (1) | 10<br>Ready, Set, Draw (2) | 11 |
| 12 | 13<br>Willow Creek Farms<br>Unit 4 | 14<br>What Do You See | 15<br>Rio Robotics | 16<br>Should I buy it? | 17<br>Solving equations review | 18 |
| 19 | 20<br>NO SCHOOL | 21<br>Assessment<br>Unit 4 | 22<br>Assessment | 23<br>Assessment | 24<br>Assessment | 25 |
| 26 | 27<br>Stock Market Challenge | 28 | 29 | 30 | 31 | |

You will probably refer back to these for your pacing in the future. You can make comments on the long-term plans as you teach (such as "make this lesson two days" or "condense these two lessons to one lesson") to remind you of changes you would like to make next year.

## DAILY PLANS

Daily plans can include an individual lesson plan (see chapter 7) or another record of what a lesson entails. Whether your daily plans are very detailed or include a short sketch, make sure to keep any student hand-outs, copies of printed materials, lecture notes, or other resources you used for the lesson. File these resources in a way that works for you (electronically, in a binder, or in a file folder). If you need to refer back to the details of a lesson, or if you reteach the course the following year, you will have all the materials you need right at your fingertips. This will save you an immense amount of time in the future.

---

*Try to take the extra few minutes to file your daily lessons (including student handouts) neatly. You will thank yourself the next time you teach the course.

---

*Some veteran teachers do not keep their daily lesson plans. Instead, they have unit plan records and then files of materials they used in the unit plan.

## Calendars

For planning, you will want to have a school calendar on hand. Print a copy of your school calendar, which usually includes school holidays, first and last days of school, and any other important days, such as teacher workdays. Also locate a calendar or list of school events, such as faculty or department meetings, professional development opportunities, minimum school days, back-to-school night, open house, school rallies, etc. Keep this list of events nearby when you plan your pacing.

### DAILY/WEEKLY TO-DO LIST

There are many administrative and clerical tasks that must be done as part of the job of teaching. It can be overwhelming to tackle all of those tasks each day. One strategy for keeping the seemingly never-ending list from overwhelming you is to create a weekly to-do list. Delegate one day of the week for tackling those types of tasks. Here's an example:

- Monday: Check student attendance records and assign detention for excessive tardies
- Tuesday: Contact parents of students who are struggling
- Wednesday: Complete and submit any paperwork
- Thursday: Filing
- Friday: Make copies for next week

Daily to-do lists can also come in handy. One of my favorite strategies for completing a daily to-do list is to identify things to be done before school, during your prep period, and things to do after school. Here is an example:

- Before school: finish grading assignments
- During preparation period: look at lesson plans for next week and identify what needs to be copied and what materials are needed
- After school: Make copies for the next week

## Taking Attendance

This daily, possibly hourly (if you teach multiple classes a day) task is not the best use of your time, but is most likely a requirement of the job. Get into a routine of taking attendance immediately when class begins. If you have a warm-up activity or other class starter, students can begin working while you take attendance. Having assigned seats and working off of a seating chart can make this task go much quicker.

Tardies, especially in middle school, junior high, and high school, can become a logistical nightmare. Some schools require teachers to keep track of students' tardies and assign detentions after a predetermined number of tardies. To streamline this, I mark tardies directly in the online roll system, and then once a week, I pull a report from the system with a list of students and the number of absences and tardies. From this list, I write up disciplinary actions and keep a record in my discipline records.

---

*Some sites require students to sign a tardy sign-in sheet upon arriving late to class. Check with an administrator to see if your site has this requirement. If students sign in when tardy, you can use this list to keep track of tardies.

---

My students turn in their homework with a cover sheet on top. They use the same cover sheet for an entire unit. I set the empty cover sheets on a table by the door, and students pick up their sheets as they walk in. To take roll, I can just grab the remaining sheets from the table and see who is absent. When printing the cover sheets I use a standard 8 1/2" by 11" paper and have students fold the paper lengthwise. Then they can slip their assignment in the folded paper.

Name _____

# Homework for Chapter 6
*Homework is due the class period immediately following the assigned date.*

| Date | Section | Score |
|------|---------|-------|
| 12/4 | 6.1A | |
| 12/5 | 6.1B | |
| 12/9 | 6.2A | |
| 12/10 | 6.2B | |
| 12/11 | 6.3A | |
| 12/12 | 6.3B | |
| 12/13 | Review | |
| 12/16 | Quiz | ☺ |

6.1A Read 344-352 1, 3, 5, 7, 9, 11, 13
6.1B Read 352-358 14, 15, 17, 18, 21, 23, 25
6.2A Read 363-369 27-30, 35, 37, 39-41, 43, 45
6.2B Read 369-382 47, 49, 51, 53, 55, 57-59, 61
6.3A Read 386-397 63, 65, 66, 69, 71, 73, 75, 77
6.3B Read 397-404, 79, 81, 83, 85, 87, 89

## Emails

Oh, the daily influx of teacher emails! School administration, the secretary, your colleagues, your students, and parents will all use email as a main form of communication. You will also notice that many companies will send you solicitations for their products. The most efficient way I have found to respond to emails is to set a specific time to do so. If you are constantly checking your email, you will not be able to focus on your students and teaching. Pick two or three times during the day to check and respond to email. You may choose the fifteen minutes before school starts, a few minutes during your preparation period, and maybe a few minutes after school.

Take advantage of "unsubscribe," "block," and "send to trash" features for emails that come from sources not relevant to you like, random educational companies. Create folders to file important emails you want to refer back to. A few must-have folders include "parent contact," "student information," and "school information."

---

*Create a folder to store information such as Individual Educational Plans (IEPs) and other student-specific supports.

---

## Paperwork

Besides your electronic inbox, your physical inbox will be constantly full. To stay on top of physical paperwork, only keep the essentials. Sometimes you will get catalogs from education companies—these you can toss (just check their website for products and services). Sometimes flyers advertising student activities (such as dances, skate nights, etc.) will pop into your box. Post these in your room where students can see them and only keep them up until the event date. Some paperwork will just need your signature; in these cases, bring a pen with you to the main office (or wherever your mailbox is) so you can sign and return them right then.

The most critical paperwork is confidential student paperwork. This includes learning plans, discipline plans, and other personal information. Keep these papers filed in a binder or manila folder and put them in a secure location. Do not leave confidential paperwork anywhere students may see it (for example, laying out in the open on your desk).

Be very selective about what you keep. When you pick up your mail from the school office, throw away anything you don't need before you even return to your classroom. Make sure to clearly label files and keep only papers you will need to reference again.

## COMMUNICATION RECORDS WITH PARENTS

It is vital to keep records of all communication with parents, especially when communicating about low grades or behavior concerns. Most parents can be reached through email, which makes this record keeping a lot easier. Just keep a copy of your sent email and file it in a "parent communication" folder. If you notice you are communicating a lot with one parent, create a subfolder under "parent contact" with the student's initials or other coded labels.

---

*Do not send emails or create physical or electronic folders with students' names on the label. Instead, use initials or another coding system. This keeps sensitive student information more confidential.

---

If there is a case where you phone a parent or have an in-person or online conference, keep notes of these instances and what the conversation entailed. File these physical documents or create and file electronic copies.

## STUDENT HANDOUTS AND OTHER LESSON MATERIALS

Having a system to file student handouts and lesson materials (such as lecture notes) is key to saving yourself a ton of time next school year. Think of the time you take to organize handouts and other lesson materials as an investment in your future self. All of the things you created this year will be built upon in the coming years. Decide if you are an electronic, binder, or folder filer, then take the time to file.

## DISCIPLINARY ACTION

Any disciplinary action you take will need to be recorded. Not all daily infractions (like students not following class expectations) need to be recorded—otherwise you would spend your entire day recording these! Instead, if you notice a student repeatedly not meeting expectations, begin to record dates and times, as well as the action you took to correct and redirect the student's behavior. Make sure to keep a record of any parent contact, official discipline write-ups, or contact with administration about the issue (referrals, detentions, etc.). Because official discipline documents, such as detentions or referrals, are paper copies, either file the paper copy or make an electronic copy by taking a picture or scanning, and keep records related to a particular student together. This will come in handy during parent conferences or if discipline needs to be escalated.

## COLLECTING AND RETURNING STUDENT WORK

Papers can be the bane of your teaching existence if you let them overrun you, but you can create systems for collecting and returning student work. For daily work, I use an assignment cover sheet (which I mentioned in the attendance-taking section). Some teachers have students pick up their graded papers from a file or basket while other teachers keep papers from a smaller group of students in a folder and then return the folder to one student to distribute. Find a system that works for you.

---

*When returning student work, be mindful of student confidentiality. Always hand assessments back directly to the students, and do not allow students to see each other's assessment scores.

---

## RECORDING STUDENT WORK

Depending on how you structure your lessons and student assignments, you may be bombarded with student work in the form of papers, projects, and other assessments. Devise a plan for how you will record the work. Will you grade on participation or completeness, or will it be for accuracy? Will you keep records in a physical (paper) grade book or strictly in an electronic grade book . . . or will you do both? Will you enter in individual assignments or group them (for example, include all homework from a unit as one grade and add all the individual assignments together to formulate the grade)? Come up with a plan before you assign the work.

---

*You do not need to record every piece of work a student turns in. Some work will be practice, and some will be a type of formative assessment. Focus on recording things that truly reflect student learning.

---

## HALL PASS RECORD

Students will most likely need a hall pass to leave your class and wander the campus during scheduled class time. Some schools have a general policy on when and how hall passes can be used and what the hall pass physically looks like (some schools use clipboards with the room number on it, lanyards with the teacher's name, or planner books with a sign-out section). If your school doesn't have a policy, determine how you will keep track of when students leave and where they are. This is a safety issue. If an emergency happens when a student is out of the classroom, you will need to know where they are and how to notify them or site administrators to keep the student safe.

For keeping track of which students use hall passes, some teachers use a sign-in/sign-out form by the door and have a physical object the student takes with them while out of the classroom. There are also digital sign-in/ sign-out forms that can be used on a tablet or on students' phones. It is important to keep track of students who frequently use the hall pass and miss class. There may be underlying issues, such as anxiety or another medical issue. Having a record of how often a student is out of the classroom is also helpful for parent emails, phone calls, and conferences. If a student is struggling in a class and is often out with a hall pass, they may be missing too much instruction.

In addition to leaving your class, students might come

into your room late or during class from other places on campus with passes. Some teachers will hold students late to finish a test (this depends on the school policy), or a student may have been meeting with a school administrator or school counselor. Usually, these students will bring in a physical pass. Keep these passes in a folder or storage box. There is no need to neatly file them because you most likely will not refer back to them, but if a student claims you marked them absent and they came in with a pass from the office, you will have a record.

---

*If you notice a student is excessively using a hall pass, check in with them, the school counselor, or their parent to make sure the student is okay.

---

## MAKE-UP/LATE WORK

When students are absent or have another excuse, they may turn work in after the rest of the class. Decide how you will handle this. Will you have a basket or folder where you keep late work? Will you grade it as it comes in or wait and grade all late work once a week? If the work is coming in late without an excuse, will you reduce the value of the assignment? Will you allow late work without an excuse? Have these ideas clearly in mind before you assign anything.

## SAFETY PLANS

Your school will have safety plans in place for different situations that may arise. Become familiar with these plans before you start teaching your classes. Emergency situations include fires, earthquakes, inclement weather, or an intruder on campus. The school will have plans for each of these circumstances. Share the lockdown, shelter-in-place, or evacuation plan with your classes early on in the school year. Keep all safety information stored in a folder by the door or in another place in the classroom. Also, keep current roll sheets in your safety folder. You can refer to these in an emergency to make sure your entire class is accounted for.

## MAKING COPIES

It may seem silly to include a section on how to organize and streamline your copy-making process, but it is a real thing! The copy room can become a little hostile, especially on Monday mornings right before school starts. Try your best to always have copies made ahead of time so you don't have to do a last-minute run to the copier.

I usually try to look ahead and use one preparation period or one hour after school once a week to get all of my copying done for the week ahead.

---

\*Follow copier etiquette. If there are other people waiting to use the copier, only copy what you need immediately. If you have a prep period coming up and can wait to make copies, come back. If you are running lots of copies and another person wants to make a set of copies, let them slide in and get a set done.

---

## Storing Supplies

I think of supplies as two categories: teacher supplies and student supplies. Teacher supplies are items that only the teacher uses. They may include your set of desk supplies, such as a stapler, pens, pencils, or white-out. Keep these items in a drawer in your desk and clearly communicate to students that they are not to use your supplies. Keeping your supplies exclusively yours will ensure that you will always know when you need to replace something. Nothing slows me down like going to grade papers and not being able to find my grading pen because a student borrowed it from my desk and did not put it back.

Student or classroom supplies are materials that the entire classroom can access. These include markers, colored pencils, scissors, rulers, and other tools and resources. If you keep supplies for students, have a plan for how you will store these supplies and how you will distribute and collect them. Some teachers seat their students in groups and have a container with an assortment of supplies for the entire group. Some teachers ask students to come up and get what they need in an organized fashion. Some teachers leave supplies in a designated section of the room and allow students to access them as they need them. Occasionally monitor the quantity of the supplies. Pencils will vanish, markers will dry out, and other supplies will run low. You may put a student in charge of letting you know when supplies are running low, or you may choose to monitor it yourself.

For more expensive classroom supplies, such as graphing calculators, laptops, or other electronic devices, create a checkout system and make sure all devices are returned before students are dismissed from a class. Depending on the class size and the responsibility level of the class, your system may look different. In one of my classes, I count the number of calculators that I distribute and count them again as they come back in. Some teachers assign a number to each student and a number to each device. Students are only to use their assigned number, which helps keep them accountable for returning the item intact.

---

*Before distributing materials, have a plan for how you will distribute them and how you will have students return them. Clearly explain these processes before handing out materials. It will save a lot of chaos.

---

*If you try a system and it is not working, you can change it! This is your classroom and you can experiment. A system may even work for a while and then fizzle. Never stop evolving.

---

## Homework

Refer to the following list of items that will require organization. Identify which items you will need to create an organizational system for. Begin to set up electronic or physical systems to support your organization. Decide if you will use a binder, folder, or another system for organizing lesson plans.

- Lesson plans
  - Long-term plans
  - Daily plans
- Calendars
  - Daily/weekly to-do list
- Taking roll
- Emails
- Paperwork
  - Communication with parents
  - Student handouts and other lesson materials
  - Disciplinary action
  - Collecting and returning student work
  - Recording student work
  - Hall pass record
  - Make-up/late work
  - Safety plans
  - Making copies
- Storing supplies

. . . . . . . . . . . . . . . . . . . . . . . . . . . . . . . . . . . .

# Unit 3 Extra Credit

Explore more advanced and comprehensive forms of lesson planning. One system called backward design, or understanding by design (UbD), can help you plan entire units of study.

This system, made popular by Jay McTighe and Grant Wiggins, has many resources, including lesson and unit planning templates and examples.

. . . . . . . . . . . . . . . . . . . . . . . . . . . . . . . . . . . .

# UNIT 4

---

# Growing, Flourishing, and Staying Sane

You have worked hard to create a vision and plan for your classroom. Now it's time to focus on YOU. This unit is focused on how to sustain, grow, and flourish in teaching through self-care, support, and ideas on how to get better!

# CHAPTER 10

## Sustaining Your Teacher Self

This chapter will focus on self-preservation and provide ideas for how to streamline your workload. We will take about resources that support physical, mental, and emotional health (including planning time for rejuvenation and rest!).

### Ideas to Streamline Teaching

Teaching can be very overwhelming. If, at this point in the book, your head is spinning with ideas and you wonder how you will ever get it all done, try to trust that everything will get done and that you will do it. Sometimes working smarter, not harder, and streamlining your work can help you be more productive. In the previous chapter, we talked about systems for organizing your teaching and classroom, so some of these ideas will be repeated (but they are pretty good and worth repeating).

I usually try to say things in a positive way. Instead of telling people what *not* to do, I usually make suggestions of what *to* do. This section is the exception. Here are four "don'ts" for streamlining your teaching:

## 1. DON'T REINVENT THE WHEEL.

There are tons of resources already created by teachers just waiting for you to find them. If you have an idea for a lesson, do a quick Google search and see if something similar to your idea already exists. There are many websites where teachers sell lessons and activities, including teacherspayteachers.com.

For example, if you want students to create a Venn diagram to describe similarities and differences between three characters in a book, you can look for a three-ring Venn diagram graphic. This is also true for other often-used classroom documents, such as weekly newsletters and back-to-school night presentations. Teachers have already made these materials, so use theirs as a base and tweak them to fit your needs and personality.

*Sometimes it is difficult to justify spending money on materials, especially if you are a new teacher with a new teacher salary; however, the time you save may be worth the cost!

*I usually give myself a time limit when searching for sources—otherwise I would search forever. If I am looking for something specific, I set a five-minute timer and give myself that time to look. If I can't find anything in that time, I create my own resource.

## 2. DON'T REINVENT YOUR OWN WHEEL.

You will find yourself doing and writing the same things over and over again. For example, you may send a very similar-sounding email to five parents about students' grades. When you craft an email, save a copy of the body of the email in your drafts for future use. The next time you need to send a similar email, find your original and use it as a template.

The same idea applies to back-to-school night, open house, and other school events. You will spend time making a presentation the first time around, but save it and pull it out the following year, make changes as you see fit, and you are ready to roll.

## 3. DON'T BEAT YOURSELF UP.

The great thing about being a new teacher is that you are learning and shouldn't expect to be perfect (actually, *never* expect to be a perfect teacher!). Instead, enjoy having a learner's mentality. Yes, it will be frustrating; yes, this takes a lot of time; yes, you will make plenty of mistakes. But the important part is that you stop and reflect, learn from these lessons, and try to be better moving forward. (More about reflection in the next chapter.) You cannot predict everything that can go wrong . . . and things *will* go wrong. Try to roll with it and make the best of the situation.

## 4. DON'T TAKE IT PERSONALLY.

Teaching is a very personal profession. It is almost impossible to completely separate your personal and professional lives. You will think about teaching at all hours of the day; you will have grading to do or a new idea for a lesson; you will worry about one of your students. One of the hardest things to do is not to take students' and parents' actions personally. If a student is not doing their work, try to find out why. If they are acting out in class, get to the root of the issue. When a parent sends you a hostile email (and this *will* happen), remember that they are coming at the situation from their own position with the information they have. Don't take it personally. People's actions (students, parents, other teachers, administrators) are driven by many factors, and very few are related to you. Do your best, be intentional, and be open to feedback, but remember that each situation has a background, and it most likely has nothing to do with you.

## Creating Boundaries

Teaching can bleed into all parts of your life. When you are at the grocery store or gym, students and parents will see you and say hi. Students will try to follow you on social media. Your personal and professional lives can easily mingle. In order to get some downtime from teaching and rejuvenate, you will want to create boundaries around your time and personal life. Here are a few things to consider:

- Keep your social media accounts private. Do not interact with students or parents on social media (unless you have a dedicated teaching account).

- Remove anything from social media that you wouldn't want a parent, student, or employer to see.
- Take your work email off of your phone, at least after working hours. Unless it is an emergency, try not to respond when you are off the clock (you will have to decide what "off the clock" times are for you).
- When you run into parents and students outside of school and school events, refrain from discussing grades or schoolwork. Instead, engage in a friendly manner, and if the subject is pushed on you, ask them to send you an email so you can reply when you have time to focus.

## Physical Well-Being

Teaching is a physical job. You will be on your feet most of the day, walking across campus, reaching for supplies, bending to pick things up, lifting materials, moving desks, and more. Your body needs to be fueled and taken care of so you can do your job.

One part of physical health is water intake. As a teacher, you know that it can be tricky to drink enough water to stay hydrated. Because teachers' schedules are run by bells and we can't leave our students whenever we need to, using the restroom must happen during scheduled times. This is personal, but figure out your body's rhythm, how much water can you drink before you have to "go," and how long you can wait until you feel the urge. Plan your water consumption around your breaks. If you know you have a break at 10:15, start drinking water around 9:00.

In addition to water, you will need to keep your body fueled with food. Many teachers keep snacks in their desk drawers to munch on when they find a few minutes to do so. Try to keep "healthier" snacks like fruit, nuts, or protein bars. Staying satiated throughout the day can help you avoid the teacher's lounge donuts or buying a candy bar or soda from the vending machine. Find your body's rhythm and keep yourself fueled throughout the day.

While teaching will get you physically moving, you may also want to dedicate time outside of your school day to additional physical activity. Get your heart rate up, stretch, do yoga . . . do something physical that is just for you. Staying physically fit can help your day-to-day physical teaching, make you less tired, and reduce stress.

## Mental Well-Being

Teachers make more decisions per hour than brain surgeons do.[31] Your mind is constantly working, and this can be very draining. Teachers are mentally balancing a lot—teaching content, monitoring student behavior, checking in on students' well-being, managing paperwork, responding to parents—so your mind will need some downtime. Spend some time each day in a "mindless" activity. Pick something that does not make you generate new ideas, take up long-term memory space, or require you to produce something. One of my favorite mental escapes is a puzzle game on my phone. Other mental escapes can be physical puzzles or coloring. When you take mental breaks, give yourself permission to be unproductive. Your

---

[31] Ellen Meyers, "Keeping New Teachers from Dropping Out," *Gotham Gazette*, February 20, 2006, https://www.gothamgazette.com/index.php/state/3162-keeping-new-teachers-from-dropping-out.

time "off" will rejuvenate you and make your "on" time more productive.

## Emotional Well-Being

In addition to your physical and mental well-being, teaching can take a toll on your emotional health. Because you chose to go into teaching, I can pretty much guarantee that you care about people, want to help them, and are invested in other people's lives. Even with all the boundaries in the world set up, teaching will still bleed into your emotions. This emotional bleed is great when it is positive and filled with joy, but you will also work with children and adults who have gone through or are currently experiencing really tough circumstances both inside and outside of the classroom.

There has been a lot of research done about how teachers are affected by the trauma of their students. The National Child Traumatic Stress Network calls the "emotional duress" of being exposed to other people's traumatic experiences Secondary Traumatic Stress.[32] This type of emotional response is also called "compassion fatigue" and is common in service professionals,

---

32 "Secondary Traumatic Stress," Trauma-Informed Care, The National Child Traumatic Stress Network, accessed July 10, 2020, https://www. nctsn.org/trauma-informed-care/secondary-traumatic-stress.

including nurses, social workers, and of course, teachers.[33] Constant exposure to trauma, even indirectly, can deplete your energy and resources and eventually lead to burnout.[34]

So what can you do to mitigate compassion fatigue? First, be aware that you may be experiencing a form of secondary trauma, especially if your students have experienced trauma themselves and you hear or learn about it. Second, find other teachers you can talk to about what you are experiencing. If you have a mentor, that is a great person to talk to.

---

*"Self-care" is a buzzword right now. Common suggestions for self-care include walks, bubble baths, and other acts of kindness toward yourself. In

---

[33] Tim Walker, " 'I Didn't Know It Had a Name': Secondary Traumatic Stress and Educators," NEA News, National Education Association, October 18, 2019, https://www.nea.org/advocating-for-change/new-from-nea/i-didnt-know-it-had-name-secondary-traumatic-stress-and.

[34] Kotaro Shoji, Magdalena Lesnierowska, Ewelina Smoktunowicz, Judith Bock, Aleksandra Luszczynska, Charles C. Benight, Roman Cieslak, "What Comes First, Job Burnout or Secondary Traumatic Stress? Findings from Two Longitudinal Studies from the U.S. and Poland," *PloS one* 10,8 e0136730 (August 25, 2015), https://doi.org/10.1371.journal.pone.0136730.

many circumstances, these are great for reducing stress, but sometimes the root cause of stress may need care that you cannot provide yourself. If you are feeling especially overwhelmed and down, see if your school district offers professional counseling services or if your healthcare provider can connect you with a counselor.

---

## Reflection

Teachers constantly make decisions. Every minute you are managing lesson content, student engagement and learning, behavior, classroom interruptions, and managerial or paperwork tasks. It can be overwhelming and mentally exhausting, but if you hang in there, it will get easier.

The minute-by-minute decision-making process gets easier for two reasons. One, you will gain experience making these decisions and get quicker at them, so over time they will become more automatic. And two, by implementing self-reflection, you can look back at your policies, processes, and decisions and make changes to make your decisions more automatic.

Just like scheduling time to relax is necessary,

scheduling time to reflect is also necessary. If you don't make time for it, you may just keep going without ever thinking about how things are going. Eventually, just as decision-making becomes more automatic, reflection will also become more automatic.

I reflect a ton during the first few weeks of school. As I learn about my students, I adjust my lessons. I also reflect on the routines and procedures I have put into place. If they are not working for the classroom, I will either adjust them or come up with a new plan.

During the first week of school, schedule time each day to reflect on how the day went and how the classroom policies and procedures are running. Some questions to ask yourself are:

- Did students know the behavior expected of them as they came into the classroom, during class, and at the end of class? What evidence do I have of this?

- Did students know what to do when they needed to do something out of the ordinary, such as use the hall pass, sharpen a pencil, or get materials? What evidence do I have of this?

- Did students engage with the lesson? What evidence do I have of this?
- Were students able to demonstrate their learning with the success criteria? What evidence do I have of this?

Notice that each question is followed by "what evidence do I have of this?" This data and evidence collection is key to reflecting on your practice. When looking for evidence, scout out specific, concrete examples. For example, to determine if students were able to demonstrate their learning with the success criteria, think about what you predetermined as the success criteria and then what percentage of students were able to meet that criteria.

Reflecting on lessons should be a daily part of your routine, and you can analyze student work for evidence of learning. Other reflections, such as how policies and procedures are working, can be done less often. After the first few weeks of school, you may decide to reflect on policies and procedures once a month.

## Homework

This homework assignment has three parts. First, think

about what activities you enjoy and give you a break from the day. Make a list of three to five easy-to-implement activities so when you need a break, you have a list ready. Second, come up with three to five questions to reflect on your teaching (you can use the examples given in this chapter). While you will reflect on lessons daily, plan when and how often you will take time to reflect on the class as a whole (including policies and procedures). Third, note these holistic reflection dates on the yearlong calendar in your teaching binder.

# CHAPTER 11

# Becoming Your Best Teacher Self

We've talked about how to survive the day-to-day; now we will talk about how to thrive! When you continue to learn and evolve as a teacher, you are living your best teacher life. We will talk about how to maintain a mindset for growth, explore some specific areas you may be interested in learning more about, and find like-minded professionals to encourage you.

For your first year (or two) of teaching, you will be in survival mode most of the time. The thought of adding more to your plate may seem overwhelming. These strategies are meant to *enhance* your experience, not add to it, so don't let these stress you out. Instead, think of this chapter as the icing on the teacher cake.

## Professional Development

Just as you want to encourage your students to be inquisitive learners, one way of staying actively engaged in teaching is to view yourself as a lifelong learner. Approach teaching with curiosity and a sense of wonder. Remain open to alternative ways of teaching and learning. To continue your professional growth, actively engage in professional development opportunities. Most likely, your school site will have professional development programs, and I encourage you to take advantage of these.

There are also many ways outside of your school or district to grow as a teacher. Find other teachers who teach similar courses to connect with, choose an educational area you are interested in and learn more about it, and stay up-to-date with the latest in education news and trends.

## Find Teachers with Similar Situations

Teaching can be very isolating. Most of your working days will be spent guiding your students through learning activities, and there will be very little adult interaction. Since most of your time during school hours is spent making decisions and reflecting alone, it is important to find people outside of your classroom to connect with. In addition to the people mentioned early on in the book, site coworkers, and social media groups, a great place to find people working through the same issues as you are is in a professional organization.

Whichever subject area or grade level you teach, there is a professional organization to support you. Here are a few examples. (These organizations are based in the United States, but if you are in another country, you can search your geographic area for a similar group.)

- English: National Council of Teachers of English (NCTE)
- Mathematics: National Council of Teachers of Mathematics (NCTM)
- Social Science: National Council for the Social Studies (NCSS)
- Science: National Science Teacher Association (NSTA)
- World Languages: American Council on the Teaching of Foreign Languages (ACTFL)
- Art: National Art Education Association (NAEA)
- Music: National Association for Music Education (NAfME)

The organizations listed above are national orga-nizations, but there are also many state and local organizations too. A quick Google search can help you locate a professional organization near you. Most orga-nizations host conferences and other events for teachers to network and learn from each other. Many also have magazines or other publications to share ideas.

## Choose a Focus of Interest

In addition to finding like-minded subject and grade level teachers, you can also find a group for other aspects of education, such as technology, growth mindset, equity, social-emotional learning, classroom organization and management, and research. Just as there are organiza-tions designed to support content and grade levels, there are organizations for specific education interests.

- Education Technology: International Society for Technology in Education (ISTE)
- Equity: National Alliance for Partnerships in Equity (NAPE)
- Research: American Educational Research Association (AERA)

*Many organizations have subcommittees. If you are interested, check out how you can get involved. Sometimes volunteering on a committee will come with benefits, such as waived registration fees for conferences.

## Stay Aware of the Latest News and Trends in Education

Your days will be full of your main teaching responsibilities, and the last thing you may feel like doing is reading more about education. But as a professional, it will serve you well to remain abreast of the latest education news and trends. Luckily, there are many organizations that can summarize and give you the headlines about what is happening in education. Many times, if you choose, they will send you a daily or weekly email highlighting what's happening.

- Education Week (edweek.org)
- NEA Today (neatoday.org)
- EdSource (edsource.org)

## Homework

Identify three or four professional social media-based resources you think could support and help sustain your education about teaching. These resources could be bloggers, books, Twitter groups, or news media. Then choose one of these resources to join or follow.

. . . . . . . . . . . . . . . . . . . . . . . . . . . . . . . . . . . .

# UNIT 4 EXTRA CREDIT

Join a professional organization that identifies with your interests, teaching goals, and teaching philosophy. You can choose an organization that focuses on a content area or a specific focus of interest.

. . . . . . . . . . . . . . . . . . . . . . . . . . . . . . . . . . . .

# Teacher Binder Contents

This is a list of items that you have collected throughout this book that may be included in your teacher binder:

- Classroom Vision (from chapter 1)
- Classroom Expectations (from chapter 2)
- List of Supplies (from chapter 3)
- School Calendars
- List of Contacts
- List of Procedures and Routines (from chapter 4)
- Discipline Plan (from chapter 4)
- "Frequently Asked Questions" list of topics you will need to communicate with parents (from chapter 5)
- Plan for how to communicate information (from chapter 5)

- Mentor information or list of possible mentors (from chapter 6)
- Lesson plan template (from chapter 7)
- Grading policy (Chapter 8)
- List of 3-5 activities you can use to destress (Chapter 10)

# CONCLUSION

As you begin your teaching career, you will discover more and more about yourself as both a teacher and a person. This book is just an introduction to the many aspects of teaching. As you teach, be open to change, challenge, and growth! Thank you for choosing a career in teaching, and please reach out to me with any questions or comments. I can be found at teacheredspace.com. I look forward to hearing about the wonderful things you do as a teacher! For more resources check out teacheredspace.com.

# ACKNOWLEDGEMENTS

I would not have had the perspective to write this book without all the amazing teachers in my life. I am especially thankful to have worked with Carly Austin, Tiana Denny, Julia Gladding, and Taylor Church. Seeing teaching through your eyes reminded me why I became a teacher many years ago. The future of education is in your capable hands!

Thank you to Cassie Cowperthwaite, Katie Ratermann, Mitchell Main, and Logan Caywood for reading this manuscript and giving me your honest thoughts through the eyes of a new teacher. Your feedback was invaluable.

Evergreen Authors - Josie Robinson, and Roseanne Cheng, your patient guidance with me through this journey has made it so enjoyable. I wish I could go back and tell my fourteen-year-old self that one day, Roseanne, the girl I met at Emily's birthday party, would be here with me for this.

Thank you Marlyn Pino-Jones for taking a chance and hiring a young intern, and thank you Peggy Haskins for supporting my growth as a teacher and teacher leader. I am so grateful to my colleagues and especially to my mentor teacher, Jinee Sargent, and the entire math department for nurturing my development as a teacher.

Thank you to my family for supporting me on this wild journey. David, thanks for holding down the fort when I was writing and "working on the book". Vinny, Gabe, Rémy, and Lucie thanks for your excitement and encouragement. (Also, thanks for putting up with me as the crazy mom that works on her laptop in the back of the car while you were at sports practice.) Mom, thanks for helping me juggle everything!

# NOTES

# Notes

# THE OTHER SIDE OF THE DESK

Made in the USA
Las Vegas, NV
08 April 2021